James A. Rousmaniere, Jr.
1945- 2022

Swami Vivekananda
"Man must conquer this illusion and know that the dead are here beside us and with us, as much as ever. It is their absence and separation that are a myth."

– Swami Vivekananda, quoted in "Wanderings with Swami Vivekananda", by Sister Nivedita, 1913.

Psalm 34:18
The Lord is close to the brokenhearted; he rescues those whose spirits are crushed.

Mundaka Upanishad
"May we learn to be like a river that dances and sings the songs of the eternal, traveling and surrendering to the many bends, until she finally meets her beloved ocean."

"In Blackwater Woods" by Mary Oliver

Look, the trees
are turning
their own bodies
into pillars

of light,
are giving off the rich
fragrance of cinnamon
and fulfillment,

the long tapers
of cattails
are bursting and floating away over
the blue shoulders

of the ponds,
and every pond,
no matter what its
name is, is

nameless now.
Every year
Everything
I have ever learned

in my lifetime leads back to this: the
fires
and the black river of loss
whose other side

is salvation,
whose meaning
none of us will ever know.
To live in this world

you must be able
to do three things:
to love what is mortal;
to hold it

against your bones knowing
your own life depends on it; and,
when the time comes to let it go,
to let it go.

Water Connections

≈ ≈ ≈ ≈

Water
Connections

What fresh water means to us,
what we mean to water

≈ ≈ ≈ ≈

JIM ROUSMANIERE

≈ ≈ ≈ ≈

BAUHAN PUBLISHING
PETERBOROUGH · NEW HAMPSHIRE
2019

Library of Congress Cataloging in Publication Control Number:
2019015065.

Library of Congress cataloging information is available at the Library of
Congress website: https://www.loc.gov/publish/cip/

Please visit **www.waterconnections.net** to contact Jim Rousmaniere.

Book design by Kirsty Anderson
Cover design by Henry James
Cover photograph by Steve Hooper, www.hoopervisuals.com
Printed by Versa Press

BAUHAN
PUBLISHING LLC
PO BOX 117 PETERBOROUGH NEW HAMPSHIRE 03458
603-567-4430
WWW.BAUHANPUBLISHING.COM

This book is dedicated to all the water that flows through our lives.

CONTENTS

INTRODUCTION

Somewhere near where you live or travel there's a river or a stream. It could be a steady flow or a seasonal trickle or roiling rapids. If you were to stop and study that river or stream long enough, you could learn a lot about water and nature. You could also learn a lot about us: humans.

Not long ago, quite out of the blue I found myself studying a stream. The experience opened me to how our priorities and practices around water have changed over the years, and in that way, I got a sense of what water has meant to us.

In the course of things, I visited other rivers and streams where I got a sense of what we have meant to water.

I came upon rivers that we had straightened for seemingly good reasons but ultimately bad results. I toured cities where runoff from rain has ruined brooks. I looked into lakes where new species of fish had been put in without much thought to the consequences. I saw how modern science has both improved and worsened the quality and quantity of water around us. I discovered how and why the costs of water—a finite substance in a land of infinite development and growth—are rising.

This search for what water means to us and what we mean to water began in 2012 when my tiny town in New Hampshire celebrated its bicentennial. The hilly community of Roxbury, population 211, had history. Its early days included several small mills, then the town took to quarrying granite, and, after cars came along, Roxbury became a bedroom community for jobs elsewhere. There was one other distinction: Roxbury is one of the least built-up communities you'll ever find. That's due mainly to government land controls around two drinking water reservoirs for a neighboring city and a federal flood control dam that protects towns and property owners a great many miles away.

I wondered, if water could define the character of a town by helping keep it green, what else could it mean to us? Much. Our connections to water—and our connections among ourselves when we're around water—are many and complex and occasionally difficult. We fight over water pollution, the building of dams, the demolition of dams, the costs of erosion, the causes of floods, the taste of water, the price of water, the supply of water and even whether horseback riders near some reservoirs should be made to fit their horses with diapers.

The stream where my discoveries began is a half-mile walk through the woods from my home. Its name is Roaring Brook. I've seen it full of spring snowmelt and autumn rain, and also fixed in the grip of winter when the only hint of movement is a muffled gurgling from beneath the ice. Sometimes in August the stream is so light that it looks like a line of dry rocks; at other times there's enough water to pool up and sustain quiet communities of insect life; and every so often, during the hardest rains, the stream puts out a roar.

This four-mile-long stream has likely followed pretty much the same course for thousands of years, and it's likely carried roughly the same volume of water during most of that time. However, Roaring Brook's story, like most stories about water in this country, is not as much about permanence as about change—much of it recent.

Not all that long ago we dumped raw sewage into rivers without giving it a thought, for example. We used to flush unused prescription drugs down the toilet, thinking that that was the right thing to do only to discover that the drugs could eventually wind up in somebody else's water. And today we worry over problems that are relatively new, such as rains that have gotten more destructive, and chemicals and other substances that we know little about showing up in streams and lakes.

The human hand in these problems is variously by accident, inattention, or willful disregard. A confirming source for that impression is George Perkins Marsh, the nineteenth-century environmentalist from Vermont who lamented the "collateral and unsought consequences of human action" when loggers overharvested hillside forests, leading to erosion that filled streambeds with silt, a cause and effect that eventually led to flooding and pollution miles downstream.

Marsh's complaint was limited in one important way. Few crises around water have a single cause such as clear-cutting on a streamside hill. More often than not multiple things help set the stage or magnify the harm from, say, a particularly hard rain or a toxic leak—bad luck, bad judgment, flawed engineering, human error—a range of possibility that underscores the idea that few calamities of any sort can be ended with a single fix.

This book takes up calamity and error, to be sure, but it also takes up recovery. That's an important finding, even for readers who've never thought much about water. The record shows that humans can correct themselves when it comes to what they've done that caused contaminations, floods, and shortages; they can learn; they can't fully reverse every mistake but at least they can prevent some mistakes from getting worse.

Much of what appears on these pages is fairly recent, which isn't what I expected to find when I set out to study water. In fact, our experience with rivers and streams goes way back—and stories from those times say a lot about us—but much of what I found has to do with recovery, restoration, and resilience in a time of technological and social change. This book is largely about now.

And it has a general geographic context in the northeastern United States, a region that's distinctive not for crisis-level shortages that vex other parts of the country but for what its long development history, its hilly topography, and particular rainfall patterns have come to mean. Still, more than a few references in this book extend beyond the region to other parts of the country and the world.

This book begins with a walk down Roaring Brook—a real stream, not an abstraction. Its full length takes us past markers of human enterprise: stone walls, old granite quarries, remnants of a mill, reservoirs, and an abandoned water supply dam that now collects silt. I'll take you to where the brook merges into a larger stream, which itself merges into other flows on the way to the sea. I'll take you to still other waters to show what they have meant to humans of differing minds and conflicting priorities.

By the end I hope to have conveyed a deeper sense of what water means to people, how people themselves have helped cause the relationship to be what it is, and whether or how that relationship might be changed.

Chapter 1

The Course of a Stream

A journey through space and time

≈ ≈ ≈ ≈

THE LENGTH OF ROARING BROOK

Years ago, when I first went walking in the woods near my home in New Hampshire, I came upon an absolutely exquisite scene. It was a stream. The water in the stream was clear. The water washed over and around rocks in bubbling action, and in some places it swirled back on itself in tiny eddies. The rocks in the streambed were round and smooth. Speckles of sunlight glinted off the water. Ferns on the sides fluttered gently, and beneath them the tiny leaves of vegetation made for a dark green floor. The image, framed by forest, could have been a picture on a nature calendar.

I thought, *This is nature in the raw, untouched by human hand.* Only then did it occur to me that I was taking in the wilderness scene from a small bridge; of course, people had been here. I looked to the trees around me and it struck me that none of them could have been much more than a century old; people with axes and saws had been here. Looking upstream a hundred yards or so, as far as I could see through the shade, I made out a frothy cascade that on inspection turned out to be water washing over an abandoned milldam; at some point long, long ago, people had put the stream's water to work.

This was Roaring Brook, an ancient stream that like most streams in long-settled parts of America has had human contact. Some of those interactions are current and some ended years ago, lending support to the idea that if you look at a stream long enough—even a stream deep in the woods remote from human settlement—you can make out the hand of man.

Let me show you. Come join me on a walk down Roaring Brook, the full four miles of it through space and time. For a book about what water means to humans and what humans mean to water, it's a good way to start.

≈

In the beginning there was a small pond. It was formed when retreating glaciers scraped the surface of the land 10,000 years ago, leaving divots and hills along the way. The pond was fed first by the melting of ice, and then by rainfall and springs and a few seasonal streams.

The first formal survey of the area, in 1768, listed the pond as Roaring Brook Pond. The name was later changed to Brown's Pond, after a man named Amasa Brown who owned land on the east side. At some point another name was added—Echo Lake—which is a bit odd because if you shout something loud out there today nothing comes back.

In 1806, young Josiah Woodward, seeking to make his way in the world, bought land at the southern edge of the pond and cut out a channel to supply power to a small mill where he processed wood and grain for settlers. He and a son ran the operation for close to fifty years before selling—long enough to permanently tie their name to the place. Today the pond's called Woodward Pond. (The name will come up again so a pronunciation guide would be a good thing: it's WOOD-erd, accent on the first syllable and a silent second "w". WOOD-erd, not Wood-WARD. Go ahead, say it: WOOD-erd.)

The land around Woodward Pond today is almost entirely forested. That hasn't always been the case. A sheep-raising craze in the mid-nineteenth century followed by a logging boom stripped the territory bare. I've seen a photograph from 1910 that shows a wispily treed landscape. The photo frames a group of a dozen men in suits. The officials are from the nearby city of Keene, New Hampshire, and they're posing atop a dam that got built to supply the people and factories of Keene with water.

The earth dam, 400 feet wide, now holds back 150 acres of water. The full length of the dam and its immediate surroundings are kept neat and manicured. The grass is mowed short, and the trim gives off a somewhat incongruous feel seeing as how the place is deep in the woods and reachable only by a dirt service road. On a summer's day you could mistake the place for a well-maintained public park but for the fact that there are no picnic tables, no swing sets, no beach, no boat ramps, nor any people. It's remote and still and neat.

An opening on the far side of the dam sends water into Roaring

Brook, which carries the water through the woods, switching this way and that, rarely more than four or five feet wide before it washes over a smoothly cut piece of granite. That's an unexpected sight, a four-foot-long piece of smooth granite about four inches square at the ends, a curiosity amid stones that have been rounded smooth by eons of water flowing over them. It's a mystery in the middle of a stream in the middle of the woods, this length of granite, with no obvious purpose. In fact, there once was a purpose, and the purpose was remarkable. The granite helped form a small dam that a century and a half earlier channeled water into a wondrous metal device that sent the water one hundred feet vertically up a hill to a homestead—a self-powered pump that's called a hydraulic water ram, devised in eighteenth-century Europe and today experiencing a revival in economically undeveloped parts of the world. (There's more on the pump in Chapter 7.)

We move on. A quarter-mile downstream of the piece of granite, past two small wood bridges usable by hikers, mountain bikers, and snowmobilers, we come upon a towering jumble of rock. It's an abandoned surface mine where workers in the 1800s drilled and blasted pieces of granite from a ledge outcropping. The stream passes the pile of rocks by maybe twenty feet, which suggests that when the quarry was running the waters picked up all sorts of things, such as residues of explosives and the dust of minerals and the defecations of oxen that would have carted the finished pieces away.

The brook's passage at this point falls sharply and the waters froth up in the shade of tangled forest. And then suddenly the land levels out and the forest backs away to leave the sunlit expanse of a reedy pond. To the side you can make out some large trees lying flat on the ground, and then teeth marks on the stumps. Out in the middle of the pond there's a beaver lodge.

By the time you read this the reedy pond and the lodge and the dam that holds back the water could well be gone. Beavers are bad for the water that people drink—that's where much of this stream is headed, to a drinking water system for a city of 24,000 people. Beavers are the source of an intestinal infection that you don't want to get. Doctors call it giardiasis but some folks call it beaver fever. Whatever it's called, water-supply people don't like it, so they aren't at all fond of beaver dams.

Shortly downstream of this point you can see the remains of an entirely different sort of dam. It's made of granite blocks. The blocks, each of them big enough to need more than a few strong backs to move, are stacked about fifty feet across and fifteen feet high on the downstream side. The structure is called Holman Dam. It gets its name from a mill owner in the first half of the nineteenth century who earned a reputation for high-quality woodworking until, well, nobody knows precisely how or when that ended. There are milldams that no longer exist today that people know more about than this one, which is in pretty solid shape. Remote in the forest and off the trails, the structure presents the argument that not all preservation need be the product of active protection; neglect can do just fine.

The water cascades over the dam and returns to its passage through the forest, seemingly unconnected to where it just was. Upstream at the beaver dam and just now at the Holman Dam, the water had clear purposes: to support a community of rodents and to turn a wheel that ran a saw. Those purposes are now behind the water; in its journey through the woods, the water's moved on.

Within a minute the stream is filling another pond. This is Babbidge Reservoir. At about forty acres, it's one-third the size of Woodward Pond where Roaring Brook got its start. Its shape is a freeform geometry of coves, which makes it impossible to take in the whole body of water from any single vantage point. At a glance, the lake could be one of countless water playgrounds in New England, except that there are no cottages or docks on the shores, no beaches, and no party boats or jet-skis making noise and waves. On windless days the reservoir reflects the trees on the shore and the sky like a mirror, a snapshot of absolute peace. But I've seen action out there. Ducks, geese, eagles, loons out fishing. I once saw two prehistoric-looking snapping turtles in furious combat. I've seen beavers swimming. Humans aren't allowed in, but on some winter days you can make out cross-country ski tracks across the surface.

The reservoir was formed by an earth dam in 1931, when the growth of the nearby city of Keene called for added water supplies. The reservoir is named after Paul Babbidge, the longtime superintendent of the City of Keene's Department of Water, Sewers and Drains who died in 1938 after half a century on the job.

Babbidge's name is neatly chiseled on a boulder on a rise above the reservoir. If you were to look down on the reservoir from that spot, you would see a picture of purity and a testament to the remarkable advances that Babbidge had personally witnessed during his long career, which began in a century when many humans, particularly in cities, avoided public water for their own health, and which ended in a century when advances in treatment technology and public health had convinced most humans that water could be safe to drink.

Babbidge had seen this transition first hand. In May of 1898, then a colonel in the Keene Light Guard, he temporarily left his city post to lead one hundred local volunteers to the Spanish-American War. The war ended before they could make it out of military camps in the South, which, it turns out, were as deadly as any battlefield. With their fetid swampy conditions and polluted water, the camps were settings for contagion in the last American war in which disease killed more soldiers than combat.

Much of the water in Babbidge Reservoir winds up entering a pipe and flowing by gravity to a treatment plant that serves the citizens of neighboring Keene. What doesn't enter the pipe flows over a spillway into a continuation of Roaring Brook. The passage is short because within minutes the brook comes upon yet another pool behind yet another dam.

Dams—there are so many of them! There are as many as two million dams standing in the way of water in America, and no single one is precisely like another. Yes, some were built off similar designs, but each of them interrupts the flow of water in its own way, each hosts its own communities of reptiles and birds and mammals, each has its own material refinements, and each presents its own intrusion or hazard, whether that means blocking the passage of migrating fish or, when they burst or crumble, washing out houses and trees downstream, sometimes taking humans with them.

Here, then, is this dam: Stone Dam, once a collection point for drinking water to a different part of Keene but no longer in use. Today it stands quietly in the woods, collecting sediment in its pond and briefly checking the rush of water when the rain comes hard or snowmelt is abundant. The granite-block dam remains pretty much intact.

Take in the abandoned site; it's possible to drift off. Here's what I mean: there's a stone building on the east side of the dam that's about the size and shape of a modern highway toll booth. There are no windows, just two floor-to-ceiling openings, one of which faces the small pond behind the dam and the other which provides access from the top of the dam. The little building is well preserved—the granite blocks are unmarked by graffiti and all the corners are good—but for the fact that the sharply pitched roof shows bare rafters and not a lot of shingles. This condition resulted from an act of vandalism in the 1980s. Some people say they know exactly who poked those holes in the roof and damaged the shingles—a couple of no-good kids in a nearby town who never amounted to anything anyway—but no solid proof was ever turned up, so no charges were ever filed.

When it was in service, the little stone building was a gatehouse for employees of the Keene Department of Water, Sewers and Drains who turned a wheel that controlled the flow of water down a pipe to homes and businesses, tasks not any less mundane than the routine functions of people who work in tollbooths today but important work nevertheless.

Going on the idea that out in the woods you can be just about anything you want to be, the little structure invites a bit of fantasy as if it were an object of lost antiquity such as, say, a post for sentries on the edge of a moat long after the castle for which it was built had been abandoned. There it is, the guard post—still on duty, forever loyal, constant, modest, secure.

Be quick about your rumination, though. Water rushing into the silted pond doesn't stay long; it ripples up against the wall of the sentry station, turns a corner, and then drops over the spillway in roiling froth. It's now on course through two engineering feats, the first one a product of nature and the second the work of humans.

The water is now in the deepest gorge of the entire passage, a seventy-five-foot cut between by two immense rock ledges, some of the exposed parts of which stand out as big as school busses.

The sides of the gorge support a variety of trees, which is a wonder given the thin layers of soil and the sharp angles of the drop and the countless threads of runoff dribbling from the heights during rains—an arrangement that leaves you wondering how any seed could get established there.

The engineering of this spectacle goes back eons to when glacial meltwater found a fault in the surface and proceeded to cut the line deep. Those were the days of huge flows of water from ice in heavy melting action—a testament to what water in its liquid form can do to things as solid as granite.

The passage between the ledges is short. It leads to a flat plain that ends at an earth wall that runs about 200 feet from one side of the ravine to the other. The earth wall, which at its midpoint stands at the height of a five-story building, was built in the 1870s to get railroad tracks across the ravine to deliver locally mined granite to East Coast markets.

The embankment was built by hand—it went up before bulldozers and steam shovels—but the engineering feat that really stands out is a granite-lined tunnel that carries the waters of Roaring Brook on through.

The tunnel runs about 125 feet. It's made entirely of stone blocks without any sign of mortar. The top is an arch twenty-five feet off the ground, and the openings on both sides have elegant stone facings. It's a work of art to my eye, but it's unseen art for most people. Unlike the magnificent stone churches and public libraries of the same era that are still in use in cities today, this masterpiece has never been on display. People on trains that chugged across the top wouldn't have noticed the artistry of the tunnel down below, and that goes for hikers who traverse the top today. The architectural gem is literally under their noses, beneath their feet, and out of sight.

Roaring Brook passes through this stone wonder and then past a small clearing on one side where more recent signs of human activity come into view: bull's-eye targets on tree trunks and then, through trees on both sides, a couple of modest houses.

Until fairly recently there were vestiges of early industrial enterprise in the stream at this point. There was a pile of rocks that had been part of the dam for the Page Peg Mill. But one day not long ago a bunch of kids went in, pried some of the rocks loose, and laid in a tarp with the apparent goal of creating a makeshift swimming hole. The tarp lasted as long as you might expect in a stream that's subject to occasional strong flows; afterward there remained no sign at all of the old milldam—a reminder of the fragility of history even when stone's involved.

A final landmark awaits. It's a flat, low concrete bridge with steel guardrails for a busy, paved two-lane road. It's a crossing that, unlike the graceful stone tunnel upstream that we just passed, is an affirmation of function over form.

At this point the stream hits a short and flat stretch, and in less than a minute the water pours into a larger flow called Otter Brook. That's the end of Roaring Brook. The waters are in a different current now, heading on to merge with other waters, on to other things. There's no ceremony. There's no sign that says this is it. There's only the flow on to other experiences.

~

FLOWING ON

In long-settled parts of the country such as New England, some waterways carry more than one name. Otter Brook, into which the waters of Roaring Brook just now flowed, has been called Otter River, and it's also known today as The Branch. (You don't say "Branch." You say "The Branch." On some old maps, it's also called The North Branch to distinguish it from The East Branch, a stream of water into which it will shortly merge that's also called the Minnewawa, a word that comes from the Ojibway language and means "pleasant sound.")

Otter Brook (a.k.a. The Branch, The North Branch) is a rushing stream that can carry twenty to thirty times the volume of water that comes in from Roaring Brook, depending on the season. A gauge at the Otter Brook federal flood control dam upstream puts the flow at up to several hundred cubic feet per second. State Fish and Game workers stock the stream with 2,000 brook and rainbow trout each year, hence the frequent appearance of anglers on a bridge that crosses it. Kayakers rate the stream as Class 2, meaning moderate difficulty; brightly dressed paddlers and their watercraft commonly show up in the spring when the flood control dam releases water; they dodge the rocks down Otter Brook, through the merger with somewhat smaller Minnewawa, and down toward the Ashuelot River.

The Ashuelot is an impressive flow, and far more interesting than its Algonquin name—"a place between two places"—suggests. Its sixty-four-mile run through towns and forests of southwestern New Hampshire includes evidence of humans dating back more than 10,000 years. The watershed includes great blue heron rookeries, and the US Fish and

Wildlife Service lists it as one of its most important refuges for the endangered dwarf-wedge mussel. Its history also includes the powering of many mills, some of which got rich supplying Union soldiers with material for uniforms during the Civil War.

The river—pronounced ash-WHEEL-it or ash-WAY-let—has always come into Keene relatively unpolluted and, for much of the period after settlers arrived in the eighteenth century, it left the city spoiled by untreated sewage, runoff from garbage dumps, and dye from textile mills. That's changed now. People race kayaks and canoes through the Ashuelot's waters today without worrying about whether they're up to date on their tetanus shots.

These improved conditions now stretch the full length of the river, including past where the city of Keene's wastewater plant sends millions of gallons of treated water into the flow every day, some of that water having come from Babbidge Reservoir back in Roxbury; the water's taken a detour through thousands of kitchens and bathrooms in Keene, followed by a rigorous cleaning in a treatment system that also takes in water that comes from several city wells.

From here the river hits flat farmland, and it wanders twenty-five miles or so beneath covered bridges and by the sides of former mills, and at one point passes a place of wanton criminality: In 1983, five executives of a leather processing plant were convicted of sending industrial waste straight into the river, this after they had taken government money specifically to keep the waste out. Executives at the A. C. Lawrence Company in the town of Winchester, New Hampshire, were fined hundreds of thousands of dollars and given prison terms in the nation's first big prosecution of a felony pollution case. (There's more about this story in Chapter 5.)

Next, the water passes through some small hydroelectric dams, then an old town where mills and mill life are merely memories, and then it arrives at the Connecticut River, which, so far as rivers go, is the real thing. It's the longest river in New England, getting its start on the edge of Canada where moose roam, and ending in an area of shifting sandbars in the Atlantic Ocean estuary that's Long Island Sound. The ending of the Connecticut—"long tidal river" in Algonquin—has a distinction among big rivers; thanks to all the silt and sand that centuries of flows have carried to its mouth, it's one of the very few major rivers in America that doesn't have a port at its end.

Still, the river has been busy. Over the centuries the Connecticut and its tributaries have carried logs to sawmills, turned waterwheels and turbines, supplied drinking water, cooled nuclear power plants, provided highways for migrating fish, and carried away runoff from countless shopping center parking lots. The river has also taken in effluents from factories and sewage from cities. In the 1960s, the New England Interstate Water Pollution Control Commission awarded parts of the river a "D," the agency's lowest possible classification: "Suitable for transportation of sewage and industrial wastes without nuisance, and for power, navigation, and other industrial uses."

Public outrage led to private cleanup campaigns and government action that resulted in the construction of sewage treatment plants and strict controls on factory waste. Decades of improvement made a difference. In the spring of 2012, Secretary of the Interior Ken Salazar traveled to Hartford, the Connecticut state capital, where he remarked on the beauty of the river and declared it a model for watershed restoration. With a flourish, he called it the first National Blueway.

Praise washed in from conservationists around the country who pictured surges of new federal spending for rivers—as much as $3 billion for trail-building, and regional planning, and conservation, and tree-planting along riverbanks, and such. But critics of big government took a different view, picturing instead more controls on privately owned land and more federal meddling in local affairs. Within two years the celebrated Blueways program was unceremoniously scrapped.

The end didn't set things back on the Connecticut River, it only slowed the movement forward. An array of state agencies, environmental groups, and sportsmen's associations press on in the cause of river protection—planting trees, replacing broken pipes, picking up litter, removing invasive plants, and building fish passageways.

For all the cleanup, the waters in the Connecticut's lower reaches will never come close to the purity of the starting point in the uppermost reaches of Roaring Brook. Too much has happened along the way. Too much history. Innocence lost, you might say. But the picture is better than it was only a few decades ago, which is movement in the right direction.

Chapter 2

A Drink of Water Greens the Land

How we save land around water—and what can happen next

≈ ≈ ≈ ≈

CONSERVING RESERVOIR LANDS

A little before midnight on October 19, 1865, a spark got loose in the basement of Knowlton's Hardware Store in downtown Keene, New Hampshire. By the time firemen got to the scene, a blaze of quite some size was underway, but the firemen had their pumpers, and they had city wells to draw on, and the fight was going well—until suddenly the wells went dry.

The flames, fanned by strong winds, took aim on other parts of the downtown. Quick-thinking engineers demolished a two-story building that was in the fire's path. The move spared Town Hall but only after serious damage had been done. The local newspaper described the event as "the most extensive conflagration ever experienced [in town]."

For years there'd been warnings about just this sort of thing, water for fire-fighting running out, and now here in the ruins was the fruit of inaction. A special committee took up the matter of water supplies, and shortly afterward it called for the creation of a municipal reservoir. At their next meeting the members of the committee expressed doubts, as happens when taxpayer money's involved, and they put the plan on the shelf.

But the following year the idea of a reservoir gained new life. In a citywide vote the citizens of Keene said yes to tapping into a spring three miles north of the central square, after which engineers were engaged, land was bought, two dams were built, pipes consisting of hollowed-out logs were laid, and within three years water was flowing to downtown Keene.

The supply led to demands for still more water in the growing community. Among others, companies that repaired locomotives, and businesses that made waterwheels and pails and furniture said that they needed it for their expanding operations.

An auxiliary reservoir was built on an elevated lot on the east side of town, and not too many years after that citizens called for still more water, and so in 1886 government officials went looking into the hills outside of town where they came upon a pond behind a small mill. Keene bought 108 acres of land, took down the mill, and built up the dam; the water stored in Woodward Pond flowed into the rocky course of Roaring Brook for a couple of miles to a small pool whence a pipe took it by gravity down into a valley and then up over a hill and into Keene. During the next forty-five years, as the community's population doubled to 14,000 and more and more households installed indoor plumbing, the reservoir behind Woodward Pond was enlarged, and two downstream dams were built for added reserves.

All this enterprise was for the sake of water but, in the end, it was also about land. The water that comes into Keene from Roaring Brook today arrives from forested territory outside the city limits, 2,300 acres of which were purchased by the taxpayers of the Keene over the years. To this day, those 2,300 acres in the neighboring town of Roxbury are effectively off-limits to housing and commerce and anything else that might threaten the quality and quantity of the water that flows to faucets and hydrants and factories in the city of Keene.

This is the way it goes: the protection of land for the protection of water and ultimately the protection of the people who drink it. Cities far larger than this one—New York, Boston, and a great many others—developed sources of water in out-of-town places, often first with fire suppression in mind but eventually also for other purposes such as providing residents with water to drink. The cities could have found water by drilling for it—and most did to one extent or another—but water down below isn't always found easily, and in old industrial cities it's not assuredly clean, plus it costs money to pump water out of the ground instead of letting gravity deliver it from reservoirs in higher places.

So cities and towns went looking beyond their borders to the countryside to dam up streams and rivers, sometimes flooding whole towns and buying up surrounding lands. In the six states of New England—Connecticut, Maine, Massachusetts, New Hampshire, Rhode Island, and Vermont—more than a half-million acres of land today are kept off-limits to development for the principal purpose of protecting water that people drink.[1]

This chapter is about what came of such land protections—how, in fact, the buying and protecting of watershed properties was only a first step. All sorts of activities came after, few of which were likely on anybody's mind when the lands around water supplies were first saved. For example, hiring foresters to watch out for the health of trees around water. And laying down rules about what people aren't allowed to do on reservoir lands, such as, for example, riding a bike, or taking the dog for a walk, or firing up a barbecue.

There are, in fact, a lot of things that happen on watershed lands today in the cause of protecting the water itself, such as:

- Since 1993, workers at the Wachusett Reservoir in central Massachusetts have used hovercraft, motorboats, fireworks, laser guns, cannons, and scary faces to frighten seagulls away from the shores lest their droppings wash into the water.
- In 1996, the Portland Water District in Portland, Maine, launched an ecology center that, among other things, shows children how to make miniature watersheds out of roasting pans.
- In 2016, the town of Meredith, New Hampshire, dug a hole in the ground near its reservoir—only it's not called a hole: it's a rain garden bio-retention basin that captures storm runoff from nearby rooftops and parking lots that otherwise could foul the water that people drink.

The bottom line is that the protection of watershed lands involves a lot of people, a lot of tension, a lot more history than you might imagine, including serendipity.

Here's some serendipity from my own home town. In 1949 two New Yorkers bought what was initially a summer home on a rise to the east of the protected reservoir lands around Roaring Brook in Roxbury, New Hampshire. Judith and Earnest Tavis warmed to a setting where, their son

---

1 Calculations by the author based on published data about reservoirs and interviews with water supply personnel in the six New England states; the figure doesn't include protected acreage around municipal wells.

Henry recalls, "almost all sounds of human origin were absent."

In 1982, the Taveses heard about a developer's plans for hundreds of house lots on nearly 600 acres in a different part of their woodsy town. Worried about the impact, the couple bought the land from the developer and immediately deeded the development rights to the nonprofit Society for the Protection of New Hampshire Forests. The Tavases eventually donated the land outright to the organization, and during the next fifteen years they permanently conserved 229 additional acres in another part of town. In 2003, their son Henry set aside even more family land, lifting this one family's overall conservation in the watershed to nearly 1,200 acres.

Over the years still more acres were set aside by other property owners. About two dozen people on the edges of Roaring Brook's protected lands sold or gave away land or the development rights to them, in effect building on the core of what was already saved. Meanwhile, in the 1970s, the state legislature gave owners of even tiny parcels tax incentives to keep their fields and forests in nature, meaning no bulldozers or roads or houses allowed. Today fully half the property owners in the town through which Roaring Brook flows have set aside land for conservation in this way. The result is a clustering of thousands of acres of green on both sides of Roaring Brook and beyond.

So, the greening of the town owes to many things. But the fact is that it started with a single act that occurred long ago—before the enabling tax breaks for conservation were ever imagined and even before Earnest and Judith Taves found their quiet preserve on a hill; it started more than a century earlier when agents of the city of Keene went looking in the hills for water and wound up buying a patch of land to go around it. The rest followed.

Not all land protections around water arrive that way. Each case has its own context and circumstance and history and people. But one way or another each is the result of impulses to block human encroachment, the effect of which has been to keep lands green.

THE EVOLUTION OF GREEN

I visited New Haven, Connecticut, a coastal city on Long Island Sound that in early settlement days was surrounded by rolling farmlands, fields, and forests with streams running through. The community remains remarkably green and leafy today, which is quite something when you consider its place in the northern reaches of a vast urban and suburban swath that stretches from Boston down the East Coast to Washington, DC, on both sides of Interstate 95.

New Haven owes its woodsy character first to water companies that, well more than a century ago, began buying up land around their supplies. The idea that rivers and ponds of drinking water ought to be surrounded by protected lands was quite unusual when you consider the accepted science at the time. There was this common belief, for example, that a babbling stream could rid itself of any fevers that might get into it by the simple action of its own frothy movement. Here was the purported magic of "natural purification" that allegedly could dispose of just about anything harmful that got into the water.

More sophisticated concepts of water purity eventually took over, relying not on magic but instead on science that showed that waters can't rid themselves of fevers and germs on their own, and, in fact, can be quite effective at transporting them intact. The new idea was that germs ought to be kept from getting into the water in the first place, principally by barring human activity—the building of homes, the stabling of livestock, the polluting operations of industry, and so on—from the surrounding land. As a result, the New Haven Water Company in southern Connecticut eventually wound up controlling 26,000 acres of undeveloped land around dozens of streams and ponds in seventeen neighboring communities.

The accumulation of all that property was impressive, but equally interesting is how those lands gradually took on a purpose that had little to do directly with water at all.

The twentieth century was a century of sprawl and also a dawning resistance to sprawl. People in New Haven looked at what was coming, and it occurred to them that the unbuilt lands of the New Haven Water Company were protecting more than the quality of their water; they were also protecting the quality of their life. The fields and forests had helped shape and sustain the sylvan identity of the place—an identity that found full and energetic expression in January 1974, when the water company announced that it intended to sell two-thirds of all the property it owned, amounting to 16,500 acres of undeveloped land, to anyone who was interested.

The company explained that it needed money for water filters that the state government was ordering it to install for safety purposes. The money had to come from somewhere, so why not from selling real estate that by one estimate could fetch $32 million—$160 million in today's dollars— and that probably wouldn't be needed anyway once the filtering system was in place?

There was outrage—Connecticut's attorney general blasted the company for its "public-be-damned arrogance"[2]—followed by organized resistance and then a transformation. By an act of the Connecticut legislature, the private New Haven Water Company that had been supplying water to locals since 1849 wound up in the hands of a nonprofit regional water authority. The new owner had enough borrowing muscle to pay for the filtering equipment without selling any property, and, in fact, in the years since it has expanded its holdings of watershed land.

Meanwhile, to guarantee that no similar threat would ever surface again, the legislature enacted tough new rules about how and when water companies in Connecticut could dispose of their property. In time the state went beyond merely discouraging the sale of land around water to actually help finance the conservation of it. In 1998 the government of Connecticut issued its first watershed land acquisition grant—a $450,000 contribution to help buy 414 acres around a lake in the little town of Oxford west of Hartford.

Other states started up similar land-protection efforts. The government-run Water Resources Board in Rhode Island added a surcharge to water bills that during the 1990s generated nearly $14 million to help preserve 2,400 acres of land around drinking water supplies in that state.

In like fashion, in 2000, New Hampshire's government began handing out money to help buy up water supply lands; over the course of a half-dozen years it distributed more than $7 million to protect 5,600 acres around water sources. In a frugality move seven years later the legislature shut off funds, but money kept flowing anyway thanks to a funnel provided by the federal Environmental Protection Agency.

This land-buying for the protection of drinking water ultimately drew in other parties who had never previously had a hand in saving reservoir land.

2 Dorothy S. McClusky and Claire C. Bennitt, *Who Wants to Buy a Water Company: From Private to Public Control in New Haven* (Bethel, CT: Rutledge Book, 1996), 3.

For example, in 2013 nearly 120 acres of unbuilt property along the Oyster River, a drinking water supply for the college town of Durham, New Hampshire, got bought up in a deal that had so many parties that it had the shape and feel of a modern crowdfunding campaign.

The Trust for Public Land, a San Francisco conservation group with offices throughout the country, steered the $4 million deal to completion with money coming from:

- The town of Durham Conservation Fund: $375,000
- The Natural Resources Conservation Service, a unit of the federal Department of Agriculture: $2.46 million
- The state of New Hampshire's Aquatic Resource Mitigation Program: $500,000
- The state of New Hampshire's Land and Community Heritage Investment Program and Conservation License Plate program: $111,700
- The nonprofit Lamprey River Advisory Committee: $20,000
- Donations from 115 private citizens and foundations in the area: $556,000

In the long history of conservation, such team approaches are new. They reflect the rise of land values beyond the reach of any single buyer and the burgeoning of citizen involvement in land conservation and water protection.

It's a pretty picture, lots of people pulling together as a team. But the process isn't always a breeze, as the following examples will show.

IT TAKES A TEAM TO CONSERVE LAND TODAY

In their early days water suppliers, whether they were private companies or government departments, decided pretty much on their own what could or could not happen on watershed lands.

But as time went on, the protection of land around water became a shared ambition as other parties got involved—state agencies and nature groups and volunteer river associations and other independent organizations—one example being what happened just outside the city of Worcester, Massachusetts, in 2012.

In that case, five different groups put together $1 million to buy a fifty-seven-acre property that was in line for a subsidized housing development, sewage plant and all, near a pond that fed a reservoir for 200,000 people in Worcester, the second most populous city in New England after Boston.

The city paid in $350,000, the state government donated $400,000, taxpayers in the neighboring town of Paxton raised $100,000, and the nonprofit Greater Worcester Land Trust and Paxton Land Trust put in $150,000.

The price was steep—$17,500 per acre versus $10,000 that Worcester had been averaging for property purchases around its water sources, the difference resulting from the fact that developers had bid up the value of the land by planning a housing project there.

Had Worcester been on its own, I'm told that it likely wouldn't have tried to buy the property, the price being what it was. The same was true for the land trust, a nonprofit organization that since 1987 had been acquiring or otherwise helping conserve open space in the area. "We could never have preserved the land without the partnership," recalled Colin Novick, the land trust director.

The deal went through, and the result wasn't simply the protection of drinking water but also the protection of open space for hiking trails and wildlife meadows and nature classes for children in an increasingly congested area—acres and acres that otherwise today could be occupied by a sewage treatment plant for eighty or so homes.

But this pleasing outcome didn't come together without tension. When conservationists look at open space they want to see people on the land, getting into nature and discovering the great outdoors. Water supply people, on the other hand, generally prefer to see nobody on reservoir watershed lands, in part for the sorts of things that tend to get left behind and wash into the water, such as sunscreen and food leavings and misdirected drippings of charcoal lighter fluid.

"Water supply people are slow to recreation," said Robert O'Connor, a senior environment official in the Massachusetts state government who over the years has been involved in more than a few group purchases of reservoir lands, some of which ended up with signs that said "Keep Out."

In fact, Worcester, which gets its water from ten reservoirs outside city limits, doesn't allow people on lands that it bought early on, back when it didn't need partners. The newer lands allow walking but not much else, and under the terms of the latest joint purchase even walkers can be temporarily barred if city officials say so. That condition rankles conservationists, but the prerogative's never been exercised. And it hasn't gotten in the way of the Land Trust teaming up with Worcester on other joint purchases around water.

But in other places tensions over what's to be allowed on reservoir lands can get electric. I came upon a case in York, Maine, a wealthy community not far from the Atlantic coast. The 151-acre property in question had a pedigree dating back to the 1600s, and the place had gradually acquired the trappings of modern living: tennis courts, swimming pools, orchards, even a nine-hole golf course and proximity to a long and sinuous reservoir called Boulter Pond.

In 2003, a developer bought the property at a bank auction after a prior builder had gotten in over his head and wound up a suicide. The new developer picked up the property for $1.5 million and set about planning thirty-five high-end homes with fabulous views.

Local conservationists had known about the property. A year earlier they'd joined nine other green groups in an ambitious plan to save 19,000 acres of land extending from the ocean up through York to Mount Agamenticus, a smallish peak that at one time had hosted a ski area.

The Highland Farm property would have been just right for that conservation plan, but it takes time to put together money for deals the size of this one, and there wasn't nearly enough time to put together a bid. On his toes, the developer bought the land and began designing his high-end subdivision, and soon enough he ran into problems.

His project was close to three times the size of what the prior developer had pitched to town officials, and that set off alarms in the area. In short order, the developer found himself looking down an endless road of hearings, meetings, votes, lawsuits, and other obstructions.

Sensing his distress, the Maine office of the Trust for Public Land offered an out. A year and a half of negotiations later, a sale was arranged. The Trust for Public Land set about raising $3.1 million to buy the property and maintain it.

One contributor was the town of York whose well-heeled taxpayers, over the course of a decade, pledged $1.4 million to various conservation deals, including $500,000 for the Highland Farm deal.

Another big contributor: the state government's Land for Maine's Future program that since 1987 had put tens of millions of dollars into saving lands and waters for public recreation. The Highland Farm project was appealing not only for its possibilities for recreation but for the protection of what lived there: a rare dragonfly, various species of turtle, a small fish called a swamp darter, and the endangered New England Cottontail, Maine's native rabbit.

Still more donors were drawn into the effort, including the Kittery Water District, which provides water to residents in the nearby town of Kittery and two other communities. In 1951, the district had built a 1,000-foot-wide dam on a small creek in York; the resulting ninety-four-acre impoundment was Boulter Pond. The district owned all of the shore land around the pond but for a small stretch that was part of the Highland Farm property. Early on, the water supply people had approached the developer about buying that section of shore land but his price was beyond reach. Now, however, with a new multiparty deal in the works, the chance to complete the protection of Boulter Pond became real; the water district pledged $350,000.

There was a glitch. The water people had rules about what was allowed on their properties. They balked at hunting, fishing, and trapping, but the half-million-dollar pledge by the Land for Maine's Future was conditioned on those activities being allowed.

Wolfe Tone, who had put together the deal for the Trust for Public Land, told me that he had seen conservation deals in the state fall apart on that condition. In the case of the Boulter Pond property, he recalled, "We had to go into serious problem-solving mode."

Mike Rogers, the superintendent of the water district, put it this way: "We had different recreation ideas."

The Highland Farm deal almost did fall apart on those differences several times, but eventually an arrangement was worked out. The water district wound up directly owning sixty acres of the property where fishing's not allowed—nor boating, ice skating, ice fishing, camping, tree cutting, burning of fires of any kind, and dogs have to be leashed. The purchase and sale agreement for the land runs 113 pages, and it prohibits the water district from ever building anything on the land or selling it—conditions that it grudgingly accepted.

The Highland Farm deal was one of more than eighty transactions that went into the Mount Agamenticus to the Sea Initiative, a truly impressive project. In terms of scale, the Highland Farm addition was pretty small, but memories of the deal remain hot to the touch. Summing up the experience half a dozen years later, Tone of the Trust for Public Land said, "It was hard."

THE PUBLIC IS WELCOME ON PUBLIC RESERVOIR LANDS—SORT OF

You can get to the Roaring Brook reservoirs by several dirt service roads that penetrate the forested watershed. The general character is woodsy and wild with an occasional howling of coyotes, screeching of owls, and gobbling from flocks of wild turkeys depending on the time of day and the time of year.

At certain points, if you look up you'll notice bright green signs nailed to trees that say no hunting, no camping, no fishing, no dogs, no trespassing and so on. The fact that the signs are up high and beyond the reach of even the tallest person tells you something, as does the occasional bullet hole.

In the course of researching this book, I met a lot of watershed managers. They're a dedicated lot, and generally friendly, too. By no means are they as unwelcoming as the posted signs that say, essentially, "Keep Out." It's just that these people have an important job to do, which is to watch out for what might get into the water that the public ultimately drinks, and that means setting limits on what's allowed on reservoir lands.

Despite the bright green signs that I just mentioned, people have been known to hike the roads around the Roaring Brook reservoirs, sometimes with dogs; snowmobilers use the trails and, in some cases, keep them trimmed. Local police make spotty patrols but there's no big fuss. The numbers of trespassers in the Roaring Brook watershed are small, this being a rural part of a rural state with lots of other places where people can hike or hunt or fish or bike or go out on motorized vehicles without coming upon a threatening sign posted on a tree.

But around more congested places the traffic on reservoir lands can get to be quite heavy, and so a fair amount of energy goes into watershed protection. Take, for example, the public access plan for the forested lands around the Wachusett Reservoir, a 4,000-acre lake in a densely populated area just west of Boston, Massachusetts. The rules there say no to: swimming, kayaking, snowmobiles, outdoor cooking, camping, dogs, paintball games, ice skating, ice fishing, snowshoeing on the ice, alcohol, large gatherings, target shooting, hunting in most places, bike riding in most places, all-terrain vehicles, metal detecting, and so on. The rules are detailed to the point of spelling out the precise types of containers that can be used for geocaching, a modern-day treasure hunt game that's brought rising numbers of humans onto reservoir lands. The prohibitions have come in for some criticism, and the Wachusett Reservoir managers don't hide that fact. They post citizen complaints on their website including this suggestion: "Less signs that begin with the word no."

The rules and prohibitions on Wachusett reservoir lands are grounded in cold economics, because without them the people who run the place would have had to spend $200 million to install and then run a filtration plant that the federal government insisted on, initially in a kindly way and then in court. In 2000, after a trial, a federal judge gave Wachusett a pass on having to install filters thanks in part to the attention and restrictions that the reservoir managers had placed on the lands that surrounded their water supply.[3]

The math for this sort of thing is actually quite compelling. Several years ago the people who run the water system for New Haven, Connecticut, did a study that compared the costs of two different approaches to managing drinking water: either pay for and run a treatment plant to get rid of contamination, or buy 480 acres of watershed land and restrict human activity on it. The numbers showed that it would be cheaper in the long run to buy the land and protect it from pollution that might otherwise get into the water.[4]

There's another example not far from where I live in the town of Hancock, New Hampshire. The community of 1,700 people has several distinctions. First, it's named after the signer of the Declaration of

---

3 United States of America v. Massachusetts Water Resources Authority, and Metropolitan District Commission (United States District Court, District of Massachusetts, Civil Action Number 98-10267, May 5, 2000). http://www.mwra.state.ma.us/04water/html/0500Courtdec.htm
4 John P. Hudak et al, *Estimating Potential Costs of Watershed Development on Drinking Water Treatment* (New Haven, CT: South Central Connecticut Regional Water Authority, et al, 2013).

Independence who owned land there, and it's home to a fair number of artists and writers, plus its annual town parade has been known to include a strolling cow. There's also the fact that one of the federal government's ten Very Long Baseline Array radio telescopes for astronomy research is located within the boundaries of the forested community, a massive 240-ton dish that's aimed at the heavens to collect data about such things as pulsating stars and planetary nebulae.

More down to earth, Hancock has the only reservoir in the state of New Hampshire—and one of only about fifteen among hundreds of reservoirs in all of New England—where the raw water is judged to be clean enough to not need filtering before it enters pipes that deliver it to homes and businesses in town.

That last distinction didn't come easily. In the late 1980s the town of Hancock, like every other community with a surface supply of drinking water in the country, was ordered by the government to filter the water that flowed out of its fifteen-acre reservoir up on a hill. Locals balked at the order because it would have meant as much as $1 million for new equipment. Kurtis Grassett, who at the time ran the town's public works department, told me, "It would have been cheaper to drill every one [in town] a new well."

The town fought back with test results that convincingly showed that the water in Juggernaut Pond was naturally clean enough to meet federal purity standards. The pristine condition owed partly to the fact that the lands surrounding the water supply had never supported so much as a shack, meaning no legacy of industrial pollution or sewage contamination that might leach in. Plus, the reservoir is deep and is fed mostly by springs, therefore little of its water washes in from the surface of the land. Then, too, the pond's waters have always been good and are a matter of pride; an historian in the late nineteenth century enthused, "[I]ts waters gleam in the August sunshine like a pearl on the breast of nature." [5]

On top of all that, the town has rules about what's allowed on the land around Juggernaut Pond, such as yes to hunting and trapping but no to fishing and gasoline-powered anything. There's apparently been no noise about those rules. The pond is in a generally undeveloped part of the

---

5 William Willis Hayward, *The History of Hancock, New Hampshire, 1764–1889* (Hancock, NH: Hancock Town History Committee, 1889), 57.

state where there are plenty of other forested lands and lakes for outdoor recreation.

But go further east, to where New Hampshire's population is denser and larger and where open space is a rarer thing, and you'll find plenty of tension and heat about what's allowed around drinking water supplies.

In 2014, acting on worries about disease-causing organisms washing into their reservoir, the commissioners of the city of Manchester's Water Works Board voted in new rules about horses on the lands around Lake Massabesic (from the Abenaki, meaning "The place of much water"). Water supply people everywhere have long prohibited the stabling of livestock, including horses, near drinking water sources lest their waste wash in, but Manchester went a step further: it ordered horseback riders on its 8,000 acres of reservoir land to keep to certain parts of the property and also pick up after their horses—and, if not that, then outfit them with diapers.

The step, apparently the first of its kind in the nation, followed years of debate and meetings that in one case included a show of force of 300 outraged riders. The critics' argument was and is that road apples don't carry disease—it's compost, after all—and runoff from horse manure has too little nitrogen to cause blooms of algae in the water. Said Judith Lorimer, a competitive trail rider who researched the subject, "The whole issue was ridiculous." She added, "I've been shoveling horse manure for forty-three years. Trust me, if it were hazardous to human health, I would've been dead long ago."

The city stuck with its rules. Kim Griswold, one of the water commissioners who voted through the rules, said, flatly, "This is not a ban on horseback riding." In his view, it was just the latest step toward water protection, a process that had started a great long time ago when cruise boats stopped plying the waters of the 2,500-acre Lake Massabesic and continued when the city banned swimming and put limits on waterskiing, barbecues, snowmobiles, mountain bikes, and camping, and the feeding of wild geese on the shores.

In the fall of 2016, John O'Neil, who's the forester for the Manchester water works, described the rules to a large group of conservationists at a conference in Nashua, New Hampshire. He talked about how things had changed on and around the reservoir during its lifetime. In the early days they allowed people on and in the water for entertainment and recreation; they then got the public out of the water and put their attention into disinfection and filtering; increasingly now they focus on what's happening on the lands around those waters. He spoke wearily about the struggles that had come with the rules about horses, almost to the point of suggesting that they weren't worth the fight.

O'Neil was followed at the microphone by Paul Hunt, who's the environmental services manager for the Portland Water District in Maine. The district, which is a public agency, owns about 2,500 acres around Sebago Lake, one of the cleanest bodies of water you'll ever find.

Offering the understatement of the day in a panel discussion about managing watersheds around drinking water reservoirs, Hunt concluded, "Having land open to the public can be a challenge."

JUST HOW WILD ARE RESERVOIR LANDS?

The lands around Roaring Brook can seem untouched by humans. That's an illusion. Pioneers worked the land for farming, sheep-raising, mining, and logging, often stripping the surfaces bare. And before the Revolution axmen came looking for tall pine masts for Royal ships.

Trees have since come back, thanks to there no longer being much mining, or farming, or sheep-raising, and certainly no need for towering square-rigger masts. In the sweep of history, the return of forests is recent. As for what's growing in the forests today, including the forests around reservoirs, the hand of humans is there to see.

Hike around the shores of Woodward Pond where Roaring Brook gets its start and soon enough you'll come upon hardy stands of mountain laurel on the edges of the water. The shrub, which also goes by calico bush, and spoonwood, and ivy bush, is related to azalea and rhododendron, and puts out clusters of beautiful pink-and-white blooms in early summer.

The shrubs pretty things up when they're showing their colors in the middle of nature. The plants are native to eastern states, and for a good long time they've been favored by landscapers. Early European settlers were so taken by them that they sent specimens of the flowering bushes back home to be used as ornamental plants in fancy gardens.

You might ask what these horticultural delights are doing on the banks of reservoirs deep in the woods. The answer is that humans didn't plant them there but instead created the conditions under which the shrubs could settle in naturally and grow on their own, which is pleasing evidence that not all human impact on nature is necessarily bad.

What the humans did—and still do—is periodically cut trees back from reservoirs, a practice that opens up shoreline to sunlight that low-growing bushes thrive in. The managers of reservoirs rather like the bushes because their roots, like those of wild blueberry bushes that are also out there in abundance on Woodward Pond's shores, provide a cleansing function by helping filter out animal waste and sediment that runoff from rain and melting snow might otherwise wash into the water.

There's one thing more I should say before leaving this subject, a curious thing really, which is that the leaves of the beautiful flowering mountain laurel that I was just talking about are toxic. In some farming regions a variant of the shrub goes by the name of "sheepkill." As to what happens to humans who drink water that's been lapping up against shores where something called sheepkill is growing, well, the answer is, first, that laurel keep most of their leaves on year-round, and second, if by chance one or another leaf gets into a reservoir that's holding millions upon millions of gallons of water, there's simply not be enough of it to poison the whole lake. Hydrologists have a saying that I'll put in quotes right here because it has such a fine cadence to it: "The solution to pollution is dilution."

There's one more thing that you would notice out there around the water. The trees that immediately encircle the Roaring Brook reservoirs are almost entirely evergreens. There are few leaf-bearing trees to be seen. Why no oaks? No birches? No poplars? No maples?

A great many decades ago government workers planted thousands upon thousands of white pine seedlings around the reservoirs because pines, unlike leaf-bearing trees, keep most of their vegetation on their branches year-round, which means that the needles intercept rain in all seasons with the effect of reducing the volume of rain and snow that falls to the forest floor that can wash sediment and whatever else happens to be on the ground into the drinking water supply, for example, decomposing leaves that can turn water the color of tea and the taste to cucumber or fish, which can bring complaints from people who drink it.

So, humans have a hand in what grows on the lands around Roaring Brook's waters, and also what doesn't grow. Humans aren't the only shapers of those lands, to be sure. Insects, some of them accidentally introduced by humans, chomp their way through the canopy. Blights sweep through, taking out elms, chestnuts, hickories. Storms bluster in. Ice in winter bends trees to breaking. Lightning sets fires going. Droughts happen. Extinctions happen. Adaptations occur.

It would be accurate to say that not much of anything is permanent on the lands through which streams flow. It's just that, when humans get involved, the changes can come faster and in greater variety and magnitude, which can lead to surprise and strife. This is to say that protecting land in the cause of protecting water can get complicated.

Southwest of Roaring Brook about forty miles is a showcase of land protection in service to water. The spot, in north central Massachusetts, is the preserve surrounding Quabbin Reservoir—variously "meeting of the waters" or "crooked streams" from the Nipmuck—at 25,000 acres one of the largest bodies of unfiltered drinking water in the nation.

The water in the 412 billion-gallon Quabbin is close to pure because almost all of the land in the ninety-square-mile preserve that wraps around it has nothing on it but trees, hence nothing on the order of septic tank leaks or factory effluent or spilled gasoline running across pavement to pollute it.

On a map, the Quabbin reservation is an oblong mass of blue and green running twenty miles north-to-south. It's off-limits to development now, but that was not always so. There used to be quite a few houses there, including sections of land that are now under water.

Before the Quabbin dams went up, both sides of the Swift River supported neighborhoods, shops, schools, and post offices in four separate towns that, in their time, put the water to use. There'd been water-powered mills and distilleries there, along with ponds from which winter ice was harvested for sale in New York, and so on.

But all that activity got sealed up in memory in the 1920s when the state began seizing property in the towns of Enfield, Dana, Prescott, and Greenwich—little towns, modest pockets of society and enterprise and history.

The several thousand humans who lived there were made to move elsewhere, and the 7,613 occupants of more than thirty cemeteries were given new resting places. Not a footstool was left—all so that two and a half million people in Boston and fifty other communities could have water to drink. That's progress, as defined by the winners.

In the sequence of things, life didn't disappear from the Swift River area. It merely took on different expression. Today the backed-up waters of the Swift River contain trout and small-mouth bass and landlocked salmon that would otherwise not be swimming in such numbers or any numbers at all in the middle of the increasingly suburbanized Commonwealth of Massachusetts.

And humans who might otherwise have to go to a zoo to catch a glimpse of anything more than a squirrel or a possum can now come upon live moose and coyotes and nesting bald eagles among other creatures while hiking Quabbin's forested lands.

This pageant of finned, feathered, and four-footed creatures was not planned out. The aim of the massive reservoir project was to build a supply of water for expanding human populations many miles away. It was only after the land had been set aside for a couple of decades that it became clear what else had come of the action—thousands of acres of habitat for wildlife, enough to help earn Quabbin the moniker "Accidental Wilderness."

A nice surprise, a nature park. But some years later another surprise turned up. The forests, stressed enough by winters, hurricanes, air pollution, insects, and disease, were found to have a new enemy: white-tailed deer were overrunning the place and eating up all the young trees.

The property around the massive reservoir had been put off-limits to hunting, the idea being that human activity should be kept to a minimum around the water, so there wasn't much to stop populations of deer from multiplying to five times the densities of other parts of the state as they gobbled up acorns and bark and the buds of young trees without the risk of getting shot.

The threat was a treeless future that, with no roots to keep soil in place and no vegetation to slow the runoff, would ultimately fill the massive reservoir with sediment and other inconveniences such as algae and the natural toxins that they can bring.

The Quabbin managers looked into all sorts of ways to protect young trees from the deer. They considered spraying chemical repellants on trees. They looked into wrapping saplings in protective plastic. They inquired into sterilizing female deer. They studied the idea of putting up millions of dollars' worth of fences. They discussed bringing in sharpshooters. They weighed the idea of importing wolves and mountain lions to keep the deer herds down. They looked into capturing deer and depositing them elsewhere. They eventually settled on public hunts.

The decision set friends against each other, hunters versus nonhunters, and humans who believed in a hands-off approach against those who said that society's hands were already all over nature so why not get in there right now and solve the problem?

The first hunt, in 1991, took down 575 deer, and the next year 724. In following years, as the hunters did their job, the hunting seasons were shortened to two days and the cullings slipped to under one hundred per year. The tree damage done by deer declined, and the endangered forests around Quabbin Reservoir started coming back.

So the hunting strategy worked for the Quabbin reservoir, and you could say that it probably worked for the deer, too, since the hunting aligned the size of the herds to the food supply and reduced the chances of deer dying from starvation or getting hit by cars if any of them went looking for food outside the reservoir preserve.

Still, among some humans hunting is a hot-button thing, and the officials who arrange for deer hunting on reservoir lands are sensitive to that fact. They take pains to explain that this is about a larger purpose, not taking down Bambi's mother.

In Rhode Island, the smallest state in New England, there's the Scituate Reservoir, a 3,400-acre lake that supplies 60 percent of the drinking water in the state. The lake was formed in the 1920s when the North Branch of the Pawtuxet River was dammed up just west of Providence, the state's capital and largest city. The reservoir project, which includes thousands of acres of protected forests, dislodged humans from their homes, farms, and schools, and it also left deer free to browse in worry-free fashion since the lands were shut off to hunting.

In time, just as at Quabbin, the population of deer expanded, and that raised a host of unexpected problems.

By consuming saplings, the deer disturbed the lives of birds that prefer their nests on shaded ground, and they also inconvenienced birds that like their nests in mid-size trees. The deer ate exotic plants such as Lady

Slipper and Trillium but left untouched invasives such as Garlic Mustard and Glossy Buckthorn that apparently weren't to their taste. Then, too, deer brought personal hazards to Rhode Islanders, including ticks that carry Lyme disease, and hazards on roads, where each year more than 1,000 deer die in collisions with cars and trucks.

In 2010, the state of Rhode Island began fencing off parts of its reservoir property to protect the flora from deer, and it also opened the acreage to hunting. There was outrage and criticism, to which the people in charge made a point of explaining that this was about protecting the natural environment and certainly not about anybody having fun. It's not called hunting; it's called deer management.

As for the watershed lands around Roaring Brook, they're officially off-limits to hunting. It says so right there on bright green signs that are posted high on trailside trees. Still, gunshots occasionally ring out during deer season in autumn. There are reasons that this goes on, one of them having to with what it might take to police no-hunting rules on all the acres of government-owned land. And then there are the sensitivities that can come up among locals who used to hunt out there with Dad and Uncle Jack and who now wonder in a telephone call or two or three to the public works departments just where the heck society is going with those no-hunting signs out there.

Well, on this particular matter society is going in the direction of watching out for its waters, which means watching out for the lands around those waters, which includes watching out for what people do on those lands.

Chapter 3

How an Orchid Stopped a River, and Other Stories

≈ ≈ ≈ ≈

HYDRO LAND

If you were to head into the woods in northern New England in midsummer you might luck upon a puff of tiny white flowers atop a little green stem. It's a wild orchid. The botanical name is *Platanthera flava,* but most folks call it the tubercled orchid.

The tubercled's small root system is suited to moist soils, which helps explain why the plant tends to show up on the edges of streams, ponds, and bogs. It's been recorded as far south as Georgia and west to Minnesota, but its principal territory is the Northeast where the dainty plant is considered special enough to worry about.

There are twelve recorded colonies of tubercleds in New Hampshire, an accounting that tells you that somebody's watching out for them. None of the orchids is around Roaring Brook, but the moist conditions around parts of the stream are right, and some day winds could conceivably blow some of the plant's dusty seeds this way to settle. Still, the tubercled is worth a mention here for its place in a story about how hydropower, the largest source of renewable energy in the nation, came to cause the permanent conservation of hundreds of thousands of acres of land.

For quite some time one of the largest colonies of the tubercled in New England could be found near a short reach of the Deerfield River in southern Vermont, about fifty miles west from where I live. This particular section of the river went dry for much of the year beginning in 1923 after a power company built what was then the largest earth dam in the world to supply water to a hydro plant in Whitingham, a little town that in travel books is known as the birthplace of Brigham Young, the Mormon.

The Harriman dam, 215 feet high and 1,250 feet wide, flooded 2,000 acres of farmland, front yards, homes, and cemeteries. It's part of a network of ten hydro installations on the river as it runs south into Massachusetts to merge with the Connecticut, the longest and largest river in New England.

The Harriman hydro station isn't right there at the dam, but instead does its work two and a half miles away; water behind the dam gets to the power station via a pipe, and a short distance after running through the turbines the water is delivered back into the river so that it can generate still more electrical power at other facilities downstream—a repeating sequence that validates an idea central to the thinking of hydropower people, which is that water is one thing that never tires out.

One effect of the diversion of water at the Harriman project was to reduce the flow of water in the Deerfield River immediately below the dam to little more than a trickle for much of the year—in technical parlance, that section of the river was "dewatered"—and as a result of this particular suspension of regular flows, the colony of tubercled orchids came to establish itself below the dam. One theory is that the orchid had been growing in the wet soils high on the river's banks when the flows had been strong and, after the dam diverted most of the river's waters, the orchid's seeds floated down to the edge of the altered riverbed and set roots there. The orchids could withstand an occasional soaking from snowmelt and spring rains but that was pretty much it; the conditions on the edge of the river made for a happy habitat.

No one apparently thought much about the colony of tubercleds in the dewatered riverbed of the Deerfield River until two events occurred one after the other about thirty years ago: first, in 1986 Congress passed the Electric Consumers Protection Act to amend the Federal Power Acts of 1920 and 1935, and, second, in 1987 the owner of the Harriman power station began preparing for a relicensing of its ten hydro operations down the full length of the Deerfield River.

Until that point, government regulation of hydroelectric plants focused almost entirely on how much power was produced and how that power was transmitted to markets. The new rules in 1986 reflected fresh priorities: regulators now would have to give as much weight to the impact of hydro operations on the environment as they did to the production and supply of electrical power.

The relicensing of the hydro stations down the Deerfield River required, therefore, that the dewatered sections of the river start carrying a minimum flow of water year-round. After all, that was the way that things were before the dam went up, with fish swimming in the river and all. The change had consequences, first to the power company and second to the orchids. For the power company, reduced flows of water into its turbines would mean less electricity, hence less income—that's a cost of doing business in a regulated industry. As for the tubercleds that had taken up residence in the soils of the dewatered river bed, they'd be swept away once the river started filling up again.

In Vermont, the orchid had protected status. So, before any more water could be released by the dam, two botanists from Maine were brought in to survey the banks down several miles of the river, after which 565 stems of the orchid were carefully dug up and transplanted on higher ground. The episode made for great newspaper headlines, one being "The Flower that Stopped a River." Still, once the tubercleds had been transplanted the operators of the Harriman Dam were permitted to begin releasing increased volumes of water down the river. During the next five years under the terms of the relicensing agreement the power company monitored the condition of the transplanted orchids. Some of the transplants took, some didn't, and some new colonies established themselves on the banks of the river. "It moved around," said Bob Popp, a botanist with the state of Vermont who was involved with the project. Of the tubercled, he said, "It's a disturbance-adaptive species."

Meanwhile, in the spirit of preservation, seeds of the tubercled along with seeds of another transplanted flower from the project—*Mimulus moscatus*, or musk flower—were donated to the New England Wildflower Society in Framingham, Massachusetts. Recently, an official there told me that there's no telling whether the seeds that are being stored there are still any good, but they're there nevertheless.

As for the tubercleds and musk flowers on the banks of the Deerfield River today, they along with just about everything else in and around the river were hit with the fury of Tropical Storm Irene in August 2011 when violent rains and stormwaters reshaped rivers and landscapes in several states. "I don't know if they're even down there anymore," a spokesman for the power generator told me in 2015. In late July of that year during the orchid's bloom time my wife and I went looking. More accurately, we went tripping and sliding down steep and storm-eroded banks before giving up. If tubercleds are still growing on the banks of the Deerfield River below the Harriman Dam, they're a lot more hardy than I am.

There's a story here that's larger than the survival of orchids in inaccessible places. It's a story about how hydropower came to permanently protect streams, fisheries, and riverine lands.

Beginning in the early years of the twentieth century, when the New England Power Company began building power dams along the Deerfield River, it also bought land around those dams so to control the water that flowed into the impoundments. Eventually the power company came to manage more than 18,000 acres of land in the Deerfield River watershed in Vermont and Massachusetts.

So long as the company kept using the river to generate power, all those acres presumably would be left wild and undeveloped, but what would happen the day, the year, whenever, that the turbines ceased doing their job and the water in the Deerfield River wouldn't be needed to generate electricity? Which is to say, what would happen when the power company no longer needed all those thousands of acres? Would the acreage be sold off and put to what real estate people tend to call "higher and better uses," such as shopping centers and neighborhoods of houses?

The Electric Consumers Protection Act of 1986 helped provide an alternative. Guided by the law's mandate to give weight to environmental concerns in hydro operations, the negotiated relicensing agreement for the Deerfield river dams took out of play forever the development rights to the 18,000 acres of watershed property; conservation easements on the lands were conveyed to a land trust in Vermont and a state agency in Massachusetts, meaning that the lands will never see an apartment project, pavement, storage tank, strip mall, or lakeside getaway; they'll remain green forever.

The Deerfield River relicensing agreement got national attention for the voluntary nature of it—no costly and time-consuming litigation, which was the standard at the time. It set a precedent for a similar agreement not long afterwards in northern Vermont that permanently conserved 12,000 acres of watershed lands, and that also financed a fund that, over the course of the next fifteen-plus years, directed more than $20 million to buying up floodplains near rivers and streams, removing abandoned waterpower dams, and restoring habitats for endangered animals and plants.

In the wilds of nature little is permanent. Seasons change, species change, weather patterns change, the ownership of hydro companies can change. Even wild orchids are subject to variations as to where they grow. But here's one thing that won't change due to a new thinking and new laws about energy production and conservation in 1986: thousands upon thousands of acres of land behind and by the sides of power dams will forever remain off the roadbuilders' maps and beyond the designs of developers—land permanently preserved in the cause of generating power.

THE UNEXPECTED CONSEQUENCES OF A COURT RULING

Somewhere in your grade-school past Robert Fulton likely got a mention as the first American promoter of steamboat travel. But in fact, Fulton's influence on the nation went well beyond paddlewheels and water transport in ways that he surely could not have imagined.

Here's what you might have heard in school: On a summer's day in 1807, Fulton welcomed sixty passengers aboard a long and narrow vessel at a dock in lower Manhattan. The boat looked odd with paddlewheels on the sides. The boat, which had been christened the *North River Steamboat of Clermont*, then chugged its way 120 miles up the Hudson River to Albany, filling the air with the smoke of burning coal and introducing steam power as the future of commercial navigation. Shortly afterwards, Fulton's fleet expanded to include catchier names—*The Car of Neptune* and *Paragon*—and his steamboat enterprise blossomed.

Here, as they say, is the rest of the story.

Fulton's success owed in part to a monopoly on Hudson River steamboat travel that he had won from New York's state government. A competing boat company eventually challenged that special arrangement, and in 1824 its complaint reached the United States Supreme Court in the hands of its able lawyer Daniel Webster. In one of Chief Justice John Marshall's most quoted opinions, a unanimous court held in Gibbons v. Ogden that the Commerce Clause of the Constitution—a provision that until that time had applied only to such narrow matters as tax disputes between states—prohibited individual states from restricting trade on navigable waters.[6]

6 Article 1, Section 8, Clause 3 granted Congress the power to "regulate commerce with foreign nations, and among the several states, and with Indian tribes."

The court ruling eventually rippled well beyond riverboat monopolies. For example, the Civil Rights Act of 1964 that, among other things, outlawed discrimination in public accommodations such as hotels, is based on the ruling's definition of interstate commerce.

The ruling ultimately gave Washington a say on other matters, many of them inconceivable in 1824 such as the types of pollution that are permitted to waft through the air and the species of fish that can legally be brought from one state to another and laws that ordinary citizens must buy health insurance. To critics of federal authority, the ruling in the riverboat monopoly case was pernicious overreach. To others, the decision was important for another reason: it confirmed that unintended consequences of human action aren't necessarily bad. The nation got its 1964 Civil Rights Act out of that 1824 decision that was grounded in interstate commerce, for example.

There was one other impact from the ruling that's particularly relevant to this book. The decision in Gibbons v. Ogden also brought about the permanent conservation of tens of millions of acres of land east of the Mississippi, including an 800,000-acre preserve of majestic mountains, forests, rivers, and streams in the White Mountain National Forest in New Hampshire and Maine.

Today that vast expanse of federal land is a hiker's paradise and a major source of tourism revenue through the hotels and inns and ski areas around it. Go there and you'll find a striking freshness to the air, a sharper shade of blue in the sky and forests that seem greener than they are back home.

Just over a century ago that particular part of the country was quite different: a wasteland of clear-cut uplands, fire-swept expanses, smoke-filled air, and rivers choked with silt. Blame the logging industry for much of that. Following forestry practices of the time, woodsmen harvested what was growing and left hillsides a mess, unconcerned that the brush they'd left behind might catch fire and burn everything else—roots, grasses, and so on—leaving nothing to slow the erosion that came from rain and snowmelt that ultimately choked valley streams and rivers with sediment.

George Perkins Marsh, a Vermonter, had warned of such things. In 1862, he published *Man and Nature; or, Physical Geography as Modified by*

Human Action, a classic in conservation literature. I recommend the book for its heat and eloquence. Commenting on the damage from denuded hillsides that he'd seen in his own country and in Europe, where he'd traveled widely, Marsh complained about the "destructive agency of man" in nature.

Not long after Marsh spoke out, some downstate New Yorkers began connecting the flooding and sedimentation of their rivers to logging and mining practices that were going on in upstate regions. In 1883, the *New York Tribune* called for a stop. The newspaper opined that all that land up there "contain[ed] the fountainheads of the noble streams that conserve our physical and commercial prosperity."[7] New York's government had previously owned millions of acres upstate, but it had sold off huge chunks to repay debts from the Revolutionary War. Now, with an eye toward protecting its down-state streams from flooding, it began buying the land back. The product of all that effort today is Adirondack State Park, a massive holding of forests, lakes, streams, and hills that comprises fully one third of all the land area of the state of New York. The wanton clear-cutting of forests and mining of hillsides came to a halt.

In New Hampshire, too, the logging barons' forest practices showed up in floods. Late in 1896, rains hit the state hard, and here's what happened:

> "The Merrimac and Piscataquog rivers, swelled by the continued rain of the past 36 hours, have risen nearly to the highest mark. The Kelly's Falls dam broke yesterday flooding the electric light plant and causing several thousand dollars damage. Two boys, who are missing, are thought to have been drowned also. Rowe's island, West Manchester, was flooded and the bridge to the shore swept away. Fifty thousand feet of logs were swept from Wallace's sawmill on the Piscataquog, and rushing down were caught against the Second-street bridge, endangering it so that traffic is stopped. The railroad bridge on the North Weare road was swept away, and it is reported that four bridges at New Boston are lost."[8]

7 Roderick Frazier Nash, *Wilderness and the American Mind* (New Haven, CT, and London: Yale University Press, 1967), 118.
8 *The Fitchburg Sentinel.* March 2, 1896.

The floods led to the temporary shuttering of the Amoskeag Mills in Manchester, New Hampshire, and the furloughing of 6,000 workers. The problem was traced to the clear cutting of trees in the hills well upstream that left hills to erode and fill rivers with silt. An alliance of downstream mill operators, mountain resort managers, and nature lovers launched fundraising campaigns to buy lands away from the lumbermen, but New Hampshire was a small state with too little capital to make much of a difference. The alliance then looked to Washington, DC, for financial support, and there its members met people from Appalachian regions who had similar concerns.

The reception in Congress to their pleas for money was frosty. "Not one cent for scenery," barked Joseph Cannon of Illinois, the Speaker of the House. By today's standards that's an astonishing thing to say, but Washington at the time had no experience buying land for preservation. The nation's magnificent parks and preserves—Yosemite, Yellowstone, the Grand Canyon, and so on—hadn't been bought from private owners with taxpayer dollars; they'd been carved out of vast lands that the government had already claimed. And when those great expanses were pitched for conservation, the winning argument was rarely that the lands needed protection for being the divine expression of God, or even beautiful scenery, but instead that they had nothing else going for them—the lands were commercially sterile, containing no important minerals, unsuitable for grazing, and of no use to loggers far from commercial markets. In a word, worthless.

The upland eastern lands were by no means worthless, otherwise lumber barons wouldn't be cutting them clean. Under these circumstances the only way to change things would be to come up with a competing commercial argument. For this task, John Wingate Weeks found his place in history.

A native of New Hampshire's North Country, Weeks had made a success of himself in finance in Massachusetts before being elected to Congress as a Republican in 1905. He had hoped to work on banking laws but instead he was assigned to an agriculture committee, and in that unfamiliar setting he came upon a project that ultimately altered the scope and shape of land conservation in the eastern United States and beyond.

In 1909, Weeks introduced a bill that would allow the federal government to buy land for the purposes of preserving it. The language of what became known as the Weeks Act called for "the acquisition of lands for the purpose of conserving the navigability of navigable rivers"— language that echoed that of the ruling in Gibbons v. Ogden in 1824.

He later explained, "We had to find a Constitutional reason, and the Constitutional reason which we finally seized upon was the relation between forestry and stream flow."[9]

The Weeks Act passed with the support of Speaker Cannon and was signed into law by President William Howard Taft in March 1911. The federal government immediately sent agents into the field, first to acquire 8,100 acres of privately owned forests in North Carolina, and, two years later, land in the White Mountains of New Hampshire.

The heft of the Weeks Act eventually exceeded its initial appropriation of $9 million. In the 1930s, New Dealers spent $20 million buying land in depressed rural areas, much of it abandoned farms and burned over hills where prices had plummeted to little more than two dollars per acre. The government then paid out-of-work Americans to reforest the land by planting seedlings. Conservation became a jobs program.

Washington no longer buys land with such abandon. The big Weeks Act purchases, now totaling 25 million acres, ended decades ago. Land protection today comes increasingly from state and local taxpayers, private landowners, and nonprofit nature groups.

But however land conservation is carried out today, a major force behind it in its earliest days, in the East at least, wasn't about land at all but rather the rivers that flowed through it.

FLOOD CONTROL, STATES' RIGHTS, AND A ROAD NOT TAKEN

When they arrive at the end of its four-mile passage through the woods, the waters of Roaring Brook empty into the larger, south-flowing Otter Brook, the north branch of the Ashuelot River, one of the major tributaries of the Connecticut River. If you were to turn north at this point and walk or drive along a road that runs by the side of the brook past fields, trees, and scattered houses, back in the direction Otter Brook comes from, in a mile or so you would come to the downstream side of a large dam.

9 Address to the Society for the Protection of New Hampshire Forests, (undated, probably 1915). Found in the appendix of "History of the White Mountain National Forest," a master's thesis by Anthony Nicholas (University of New Hampshire, June 1959), 109.

The thing is out of scale with everything around it, which is mainly trees, as it rises 130 feet to the height of a twelve-story building and measures a couple of hundred yards left-to-right. The earth-filled dam is faced with crushed stone that's kept pretty much clean of vegetation.

There's an opening at the bottom of the dam that issues a hissing rush of water. The water roils through a no-nonsense cement and rock sluiceway and then splays into a wider rocky channel, and not much later the water returns to the wild condition that it knew before the dam and its impoundment interrupted its flow.

From the size of the dam and the thrust of the water coming out you might picture a huge lake on the other side. But most days if you were to get up to the top you'd be looking down at a narrow ribbon of water. The small impoundment would indicate that either there's a major drought going on or the structure that you're standing on is a flood control dam that's merely waiting for floodwaters to show up.

It's the latter. This is the Otter Brook Federal Flood Control Dam, built in the mid-1950s as part of an historic government response to a series of devastating floods on the tributaries and main stem of the Connecticut River as far away as one hundred miles downstream.

At the top of the dam there's no question but that you're in the great outdoors. But for a sliver of sand on a public beach at the far end of the lake and the lake itself, the vista consists entirely of sloping forests.

The history of this place includes human settlement from more than two centuries earlier when trees were felled and stumps were pried out to create farmland and pastures in a valley with a brook rippling through. At some point a small mill was set up on the side of the stream, and, a century or so later, a string of cottages was built for warm weather vacationers. Finally, government surveyors came by; then land was taken from farm families and work on the dam began.

The structure got its first real test in the early spring of 1987, decades after it was built, when nearly six inches of rain pounded the area in a very short period of time. The water behind the dam rose higher and higher to the point where, for the first and only time, it entered a cement-sided spillway on the west side that sent floodwaters around the dam. In a post-storm accounting, the authorities said the structure had prevented nearly $3.5 million in damages to property downstream.

The Otter Brook dam was built for flood control, but the project had a collateral purpose that helped win it local approval. When the dam was being proposed in the 1950s, Keene city officials were pitched promises of a public swimming area at the top end of the lake; the city had no public pools at the time, which meant that it had to bus local children to a mill town ten miles away to get their splashing in. With city officials looking on approvingly, the federal government appropriated eighty acres of farmland for its flood control impoundment, and at the northern end of the lake it trucked in sand for a beach that made for a local swimming spot. The beach remains in use today, but on a hot summer's day it lacks crowds. Several years after the dam went up, a new mayor in Keene pushed for the creation of public pools, leaving the Otter Brook swimming area to folks who like their dips and barbecues quiet. The federal government also bought more than 500 acres of additional property around the project that they've kept unbuilt.

Here again was water's role in the preservation of land. In all of New England where the Army Corps of Engineers has built dozens of flood control dams, the government owns nearly 70,000 acres of associated open space. Add in local flood control projects and government purchases of flooding rights on private lands, and you've got well over 100,000 acres of green space in the six states of New England, all conserved in the cause of controlling floodwaters.

Of course, fields and farmland were lost along the way, but the net effect was more acreage saved than was drowned. The remarkable thing is that the conservation impact in the region could have been far greater had President Franklin D. Roosevelt had his way in what became a dramatic struggle over the balance of power between states and Washington, DC.

The Otter Brook Dam is one of thirteen federal flood control projects in the Connecticut River watershed. Stirred by flooding in the watershed in the first half of the twentieth century—Hartford, Connecticut, seemed to be particularly vulnerable—Washington originally considered building more than twice that number of dams in the watershed. One expert called for more than 100 flood control dams in the region, many of them equipped to generate and sell electricity to private power companies.

Here was the idea of a northern version of the Tennessee Valley Authority, a massive jobs-creating reengineering of streams and rivers that would keep basements dry, protect farmland from floods, and produce boundless amounts of cheap energy. But for all these seeming boons, the plan fell flat where the dams were to be built.

No surprise, when you think about it. Most people don't like big new projects coming into the neighborhood, be they malls, factories, wind farms, or pipelines, because the landscape and patterns of life get disturbed mainly for the benefit of people elsewhere. In the case of big flood control dams, the benefit is mainly for folks downstream, often a great many miles downstream. Here's one explanation from a 1960s study:

> "At different times in the past, citizens in New Hampshire and Vermont have banded together to try to prevent inundation of their pasture, farmlands, homesteads and graveyards. The people living upstream not unnaturally tend to believe in small projects on tributary rivers, floodplain zoning, and reforestation as alternatives to large dams and reservoirs. Their spokesmen have recommended that industries and other developments along the Connecticut River should move to higher ground. The people downstream who are subject to floods seem to care less about the flooding of quaint old villages and farms. People in the downstream communities argue that the cost of moving entire industrial and commercial centers away from the flood plains would be enormously expensive, far more than the cost involved in developing and improving new farming areas."[10]

Politicians in New Hampshire and Vermont didn't take well to FDR's massive designs on their lands. These were small-government Yankees whose visions for river valleys included resurgent farms and tax-generating vacation homes for the rich, certainly not huge lakes behind federal dams designed to keep distant cities dry and supply private power monopolies with electricity.

---

10 J. C. Kammerer and H. L. Baldwin, "Water Problems in the Springfield-Holyoke Area, Massachusetts—A Layman's Look at Water in a Metropolitan Area," (undated, probably 1960s), 28, file:///C:/Users/Owner/Downloads/Water%20Problems%20in%20Springfield-Holyoke%20area%20MA.pdf

In January 1939, weeks after Roosevelt ordered Civil Works Administration workers to start scouting out where to build dams in New Hampshire and Vermont, the Vermont Legislature put $67,500 into a defense fund—$1.2 million in today's dollars—to block federal purchases of property in the state. In neighboring New Hampshire, Governor Francis P. Murphy threatened to call out the National Guard if federal agents came looking. He told a gathering of New England governors: "The states will never surrender to the federal government—even if God's child is president—the title to our natural resources."[11]

On the western shore of the Connecticut River, George Aiken, a berry farmer in the early stages of a prominent political career, agreed that floods were a problem, but in his eyes electric power monopolies were worse; they had, he pointed out, refused to string power lines to remote dairy farmers in Vermont, leaving them unable to compete with dairymen in other parts of the country whose farms benefitted from electrical refrigeration. "Of the two evils," he declared, "occasional floods (seem) preferable."[12]

The resistance won out as the popularity of New Deal programs waned and the demands of World War II intervened. Ultimately only thirteen federal flood control dams were built in the Connecticut River watershed—most of them decades after they'd been proposed, none of them on the main stem of the river as Roosevelt's people had wanted, and not a single one tooled to generate electricity.[13]

Would things have been different had all those dams been built as planned? Would New England still be importing 15 percent of its electricity, with all the costs that come with that? Would the region be better protected against the hard storms that are increasingly sweeping through? Would the landscape today be greener—or less green? Would there be fewer tractors on local roads and more vehicles with Army Corps of Engineers insignia?

As Robert Frost, a product of the region, might have put it: the road not taken has made all the difference.

---

11 *Boston Globe.* September 21, 1937.
12 Proceedings of the Governors' Conference 29th Annual Session, Atlantic City, NJ, September 14–16, 1937.
13 For an illuminating analysis, see *New Deal versus Yankee Independence: The Failure of Comprehensive Development on the Connecticut River, and Its Long-Term Consequences,* by Eve Vogel and Alexandra Lacey, University of Massachusetts-Amherst, 2012.

Chapter 4
The Control of Water
What we've learned—and not learned— about redesigning streams

≈ ≈ ≈ ≈

WHEN RAIN HITS CITY STREETS

From the waiting room of the public works department in the city of Dover, New Hampshire, it's a short walk to an enormous garage filled with trucks. Parked in the fleet is a pickup the size of a tank, and I climb in.

The driver is Bill Boulanger, the beefy superintendent of public works for whom a vehicle of any lesser heft wouldn't quite fit the picture. He powers the pickup out into the rain, which is appropriate because he's about to take me on a tour of what Dover has recently done to manage the flow of rainwater that comes off roofs, streets, sidewalks, parking lots, and other hard surfaces that are part of urban settings.

Dover, a city of 30,000 people on New Hampshire's Atlantic coast, has made a name for itself over the years. It's one of the oldest permanent settlements in North America, it was once a shipbuilding center, then a cotton milling center, and now a home to high-tech industry. Its latest distinction is that of being host to the first complete urban watershed restoration project in the nation.

That mouthful of an honor owes to a teaming up of Dover and the Stormwater Center, a research outfit at the University of New Hampshire not far away, and with federal and state funders and a local watershed coalition looking on. The focus of their interest over the last decade has been the water flowing into Berry Brook, a mile-long stream whose nearly 200-acre watershed is contained entirely within Dover's city limits. That last fact means that any pollution that gets into the brook can't be blamed on some other jurisdiction, nor for the same reason could any neighboring community claim credit for any improvement such as cleaner water and, more materially, trout returning to a stream that last contained them only in distant memory.

In 2006, after going over test results that had been supplied by the local citizen-run watershed group, state and federal officials declared that the waters of Berry Brook were unfit for human contact. The source of contamination wasn't any of the usual suspects—a factory, an ancient dump, a leaking sewage plant—but instead the totality of the built environment in the area. The bacteria in the stream had been delivered by runoff of rain and snowmelt as it passed over the leavings of modern human settlement consisting of dog doo, oil, grease, road salt, lawn fertilizer, residue from construction projects, road paving, and so on.

This kind of contamination has one of the least sexy technical terms you'll ever come across—"nonpoint source pollution." But the government says that it's the leading cause of water quality problems in America today. It's also one of the most frustrating because it lacks the convenience of a ready culprit such as a factory—*Here, you did it, you clean it up.*

Runoff's a bigger problem in urban areas such as Dover than in rural places due to differences in what happens to rain once it hits the ground. In forested places such as where Roaring Brook flows, about 50 percent of rain naturally soaks into the earth, and another 40 percent is taken up by vegetation and evaporation; that means that only about 10 percent of rain gets into streams and ponds via runoff. In urban areas, on the other hand, very little rain soaks into the earth because so much of the surface is solid; most of it washes into streams and rivers.

See for yourself. The next time you get a good rain, look at your lawn or the grassy parts of a park or athletic field and see what happens to the water: it generally soaks into the ground. Then look at your driveway or a paved walkway and see what happens there: the water doesn't soak in at all but instead either pools up or moves along.

When Boulanger began working for Dover four decades ago, the strategy was to get rid of stormwater by piping it away—initially to the public sewer system and later through a separate network of pipes to other places such as local streams and other water bodies. The main goal was to prevent flooding of neighborhoods, and in most cases most American cities got the job done. But when rain falls so hard that storm drains and pipes and drainage systems can't get rid of water fast enough, you get floods. That's what happened in 2017 in Houston, Texas, a city of nearly uninterrupted roads, parking lots, patios, roofs, decks, and sidewalks, when epic rains produced record floods—and that's what's increasingly happening in the Northeast, where climate studies uniformly show greater increases in extreme rains than most other parts of the country.

The rainwater disposal methods that Boulanger oversees today don't pipe stormwater away but instead let it settle into the ground near where rain falls. Among other things, his workers dig holes and fill them with loam, mulch, and stone; the fill sucks up rainwater, and the vegetation that gets planted there breaks down the pollutants, essentially cleansing the water as it soaks into the ground. The designs carry out functions that used to be provided naturally by wetlands and swamps and farmland, before they got filled in and paved over or built on.

The term of art for these new water-collecting structures is green infrastructure, which is quite different from the grey infrastructure that it replaced—pipes, cement channels, and such. Green infrastructure is about rain gardens, gravel wetlands, and neighborhood catch basins. As a result of the changes in Dover, the flow of sediment into Berry Brook has gone down by 42,000 pounds annually, and hundreds of pounds of nitrogen and phosphorus pollution have been cut.

The project has gotten attention—not only for the technology involved but also for its enlistment of public support. Among other things, rain barrels have been handed out to local people to capture rain coming off their roofs, and lessons about watersheds were started at a local elementary school. In addition, a 1,100-foot stretch of the brook that for a century had been funneled into an underground pipe was opened to the air and the cleansing functions of vegetation and aquatic micro-organisms. The share of impervious surfaces in Dover has been cut back from 30 percent of the watershed to 10 percent. Officials from across the country have come looking.

Boulanger says that some older public works people have told him that they don't much care for the modern approaches but he says that he likes them just fine, with one qualification.

The qualification is that the new designs have to be practical, which he says hasn't always been the case with the ideas proffered by the stormwater people at the university with whom he's been working.

"I saw some of their first designs and I knew that they were going to fail right off the bat," he says. He adds firmly, "We had a few disagreements out there."

Boulanger pulls the pickup to a stop and points to a dip in the road. There, he says, is where the university people came up with a system to collect rainwater that washed off the road. He told them that their design would be a maintenance nightmare with all the silt and sediment that his workers would have to remove on a regular basis. He insisted that they make changes.

"They came back to me and they came back to me and then I built it," he says.

But in some cases there's been no going forward. Porous pavement, for example. Engineers who lean green say that pavement that's got holes in it can dispose of rainwater quite well by helping it soak into the ground. The university people with whom Boulanger was working proposed that.

"I won't do it," he says flatly, returning to the maintenance issue. "We're in New England and we put tons and tons of sand and salt on roads." He says that there'd be no end to his staff having to vacuum the infiltration holes to keep them open and clear.

Boulanger's not opposed to all new ideas about pavement, to be sure. For example, these days when his department resurfaces some older roads it's narrowing the width of pavement from the original thirty feet to as few as twenty-six feet. There's a reduction of impervious surface right there.

And Boulanger likes the idea of keeping stormwater close to where it falls instead of piping it someplace else. He's bought into the idea of small localized solutions. He even customized a subsurface storage system of his own to collect runoff near where rain hits the ground. In 2016, when the EPA gave him a merit award for his work in stormwater management, it saluted him for the structure, which he proudly told me goes by the name "Boulanginator."

The steps in Dover and elsewhere can be traced to an EPA decision in the late 1970s to study the connection between water pollution and urban runoff. The findings led to regulations on stormwater discharges in cities, and then financial backing for technology centers such as the one at the University of New Hampshire that's worked with Boulanger on Berry Brook. Plus this:

- In 2012, the Maryland legislature enacted a fee on property owners based on how much of their land is covered by roofs, driveways, sidewalks, garages, and other impervious surfaces; the proceeds are used to block stormwater runoff from getting into Chesapeake Bay.

- In 2014, the Water Environment Federation, a Virginia-based nonprofit association of environmentalists and public works people around the country, opened a Stormwater Institute to promote innovative ways to manage runoff.

- In 2015, the American Society of Civil Engineers launched a quarterly publication titled *Journal of Sustainable Water in the Built Environment* that carries articles about concrete, roofs, highway runoff, cisterns, and so on.

- In 2016, the planning board in Dover revised its codes for private developers to include fully eleven pages of rules about controlling stormwater runoff, erosion, and sediment for construction projects in the city.[14]

If all this suggests universal buy-in by the public, think again. In 2011, a government-appointed committee in Dover proposed creating a new municipal utility that ultimately would plow as much as $2 million per year into replacing old stormwater pipes. The money would come from a new fee that would cost the average homeowner about $7 per month. The day the city council was to approve the plan, following a good many rounds of uneventful public meetings and hearings, an anti-tax citizens group launched an ambush that killed the idea, leaving the city to find other ways to pay for its stormwater runoff work.

Similarly, in Maryland's 2014 gubernatorial campaign Larry Hogan, the eventual winner, pledged that he'd get rid of what he called the "rain tax." And a year earlier a taxpayers group in Elgin Illinois, a city northwest of Chicago, knocked off a stormwater fee that would have dealt with urban runoff.

14 A sample from Dover's land use regulations: "149-14. Site Development Design Criteria, A (3) (b)(vii): "For large projects adding greater than or equal to ten (10) acres of IMPERVIOUS cover, or projects located in known areas of flooding concern, or specifically within areas with a one-percent chance of being inundated by water in any given year, the owner/APPLICANT shall submit a supplementary report that describes how the project will not increase the future flooding potential and complies with AoT requirements pertaining to floodplain impacts as described in Env-Wq 1503.09, regardless of whether an AoT permit is required."

Still, in the long run, progress. Opposition to "rain taxes" and the like doesn't so much question the contaminating effects of urban runoff as how to pay for a fix. With the right leadership and with enough time, I imagine that cities will find the money.

The public's come around to new ideas about water before, after all. Jonathan Ring provides a good example. He's a civil engineer who's done projects in Dover, most recently a day care center that was outfitted with porous sidewalks to comply with local rules.

He recalls how things were thirty-five years ago when he started in the field, back when rules and regulations about water and land management weren't nearly as numerous or green as they are now. He recalls the days when developers filled in wetlands and put buildings on top—things that aren't allowed in most places today.

In those days and earlier, he told me, "We did whatever the hell we wanted to do."

LESSONS FROM A STORM

In late August 2011, a furious storm howled up the full length of the East Coast and into the New England interior. The state of Vermont was especially hard hit. Floodwaters there damaged or destroyed hundreds of bridges, washed out roads, undercut railroad lines, and battered or swept away 3,500 homes. A federal fish hatchery at the heart of a decades-long salmon-recovery effort was buried beneath mud and silt. Losses in that one rural state totaled hundreds of millions of dollars.

There were lessons from Tropical Storm Irene, the first being that some storms are far worse than others. Another was that nature, left on its own, can limit the damage from those storms.

Most of Vermont was rampaged by floodwaters from the hard rains of Irene, but one town survived the storm remarkably untouched. The protection didn't come from a particular dam or a strategically located set of berms but rather something far more mundane. The town of Middlebury, population 6,500, owed its happy outcome to swamps.

If your image of a swamp is a place that's wet, scrubby, tangled, and no place for a picnic, you have a sense of much of the land just upstream of Middlebury by the side of Vermont's longest river.

That river, Otter Creek, arrives at these swamps having gotten its start at the bottom of the state and then flowing generally north for about one hundred miles, defining town boundaries along the way. The creek's route takes it past the foothills of the Green Mountains, alternately flat and steep, then to Rutland, the state's third-largest city with 17,000 people, and after that it heads to the college town of Middlebury about thirty miles away. Rutland and Middlebury are located on the same river, but they experienced the rains from Tropical Storm Irene in radically different ways.

Consider the math. At the height of that storm Otter Creek and other streams carried 16,000 cubic feet of water per second through Rutland— far above the normal seasonal flow and enough to paralyze parts of the city with record floods. Yet downstream in Middlebury, the peak flow on this same river in the same storm was by one measure only 6,000 cubic feet per second, barely enough to interrupt the rhythm of life.

Why the difference? Answer: The Otter Creek swamps between the two towns where 1,000 acres of wetlands and unbuilt floodplains essentially sucked up the river's overflowing waters like a sponge and then gradually released them over the following week; the peak flow of water in Middlebury happened a full six days after the peak in Rutland because the natural processing of floodwaters took that much time.

Several years after Tropical Storm Irene, graduate students at the University of Vermont did a study of the economic impact of the wetlands upstream of Middlebury and concluded that they prevented $1.8 million in damages in just that one storm. And that was only the averted damage to homes and businesses; the calculations didn't include what it might have taken to repair roads and bridges had the swamps not done their job.

All this put swamps in new light for me, having grown up picturing them as smelly insect-ridden places where one-eyed ogres lived—not by any stretch of the imagination beneficial creations of nature.

There was one other surprising thing about the Otter Creek swamp, and that was that they existed at all in 2011.

From their earliest settlement days, Vermonters routinely filled in swamps, wetlands, and floodplains for ostensibly productive purposes. Upstream of Middlebury they'd drained some of the wetter areas and built earth berms to create new farmland and support commercial cultivation of cedar forests. Still, for whatever reason, most of those lands in and around those swamps had remained as nature had created them: soft.

Over the years, Vermonters in other places had altered the shapes of streams and the lands around them. Upstream of Rutland, for example, they'd filled in floodplains to make room for development; they'd dredged the brooks and streams in the watershed and built berms to keep water off the land; they'd straightened rivers and pushed gravel up on the sides, one effect being to deliver the full force of any floodwaters downstream to the streets and homes and shops of Rutland. These practices, which occurred as recently as the 1970s, were widespread, leaving more than 70 percent of rivers in this one rural state unnaturally straight. There were reasons. Surveyors for roads and railroads that ran parallel to rivers preferred straight lines, not meandering routes. The people who floated logs to sawmills favored straight rivers, not curving ones where logs could easily jam. People who built their homes in low-lying areas near rivers liked their yards and basements dry.

The settlers and their successors used muscle, shovels and machines to cut off whole stretches of rivers from their surrounding floodplains. They had helpers, including the explosives department of the E. I. du Pont de Nemours & Company of Wilmington, Delaware. In 1935, the company took out an advertisement in *American Farmer* magazine that pitched a forty-eight-page book titled *Ditching with Dynamite* with the following instruction:

> "Crooked streams are a menace to life and crops in the areas bordering their banks. The twisting and turning of the channel retards the flow and reduces the capacity of the stream to handle large volumes of water. Floods result. Crops are ruined. Lives are lost. Banks are undermined, causing cave-ins that steal valuable acreage . . .
>
> "Dynamite may be used most effectively in taking out the kinks in a crooked stream."[15]

The blasting and digging and straightening of rivers in Vermont had consequences. Stormwaters in straight and deep channels tend to flow faster than waters in meandering and shallow streams that can overflow onto surrounding lands; when stormwaters are confined to engineered

15 Advertisement in *American Farmer*, August 1935, 385.

channels, they tend to hurtle downstream with force enough to take out the foundations of roads and lift whole bridges out of place —- just the sort of things that occurred during Tropical Storm Irene. No surprise to those who had done their reading and understood what Gilbert White, a prominent geographer in Chicago, had written more than sixty years earlier. "Floods are 'acts of God,'" he wrote, "but flood losses are largely acts of man."

Earlier than elsewhere, Vermonters began looking to nature to help avoid or minimize flood losses. Some of them were likely inspired by Paul Sears, an ecologist who during the 1950s chaired one of the country's first graduate programs in conservation, at Yale. In 1955, he presented an ambitiously titled paper at an international symposium in Princeton, New Jersey—"Man's Role in Changing the Face of the Earth"—that suggests that he might have a thing or two to say to the duPont explosives people:

> "Far greater funds are expended upon efforts to control flood *after* water has reached the river channels than are devoted to securing proper land use on the tributary uplands to retain the water where it falls. This is an interesting aspect of a technological culture where emphasis is on engineering rather than on biological controls."[16]

In time, the idea of keeping hands off nature began to make its way into government policy. In the 1990s, Vermont's state government began laying down rules against cutting off rivers from their floodplains; the rules said no to reshaping rivers and streams into rock-lined channels; better to let rivers occasionally soak into their floodplains.

But change can come hard. In the days immediately following Tropical Storm Irene in 2011, local officials in towns across Vermont sent in the bulldozers to clean out streams and rivers. They dug out streams to make them deeper, and in the process harvested gravel to use for road repairs. State regulators, cut off by the storm, were unable to stop the surgery. In a post-mortem, one state senator described Vermont as having been "a lawless state."

The government responded with still stiffer limits on altering the

---

16 The passage appears in "Processes of Environmental Change by Man" in *Man's Role in Changing the Face of the Earth*, ed. William. L. Thomas Jr. (Chicago: Wenner-Gren Foundation, University of Chicago Press, 1956), 480.

shapes of streams, and it also passed tax breaks and other incentives to encourage landowners to keep their streamside properties unbuilt and able to soak up future rains and floodwaters—just as the unbuilt swamps around Otter Creek had done naturally.

The state cranked up its public education activities. I have evidence on my desk in the form of a photo that a state worker sent me. The picture shows several beefy men in bright orange short-sleeved shirts standing around a low table, the surface of which is contained by edging several inches high. The surface holds what appears to be sand and little blocks of wood. The incongruity is sharp: big men with big bellies focusing intently on what has the distinct look of a tabletop sandbox at a preschool.

The setting's not a preschool but instead what has the feel of a public works garage. The table they're standing around is called a flume. It's more dynamic than the photograph suggests because at a certain point the people in charge can send a flow of water running onto the table at one end and down a course that they've designed in the sand, down past the little blocks of wood and eventually to a drain at the other end. The blocks of wood represent buildings. The sand, which is actually little bits of plastic, represents land. The water represents a river that—I've seen the thing work—at the will of the operators can be turned into a surge strong enough to erode the sand so as to flood the land and wash away whatever gets in the way.

Staci Pomeroy, the state worker who sent me the photo, said that the flume was helping get the word out about how streams work. She said, "When I first started [fifteen years ago] you could not say 'fluvial geomorphology' in a meeting without getting lots of blank looks; now more and more folks around Vermont know what that actually means."

The term roughly means the science of rivers as they flow over land. Pomeroy and others in her field see rivers as complicated things that do more than carry away rains. These people see rivers as part of the environment in which they exist, connected to land on both sides, upstream and downstream. They see rivers as animate objects: changeable, moody, and unpredictable, and not given to being controlled. The way they look at it, *we* are the ones who ought to be controlled, both in what we do and don't do to the lands around rivers and also in what we do and don't do to the rivers that flow through those lands.

For quite some time this sort of thinking about rivers and land was pretty much confined to the offices of government environmental workers. They could pass roads and highway people in the hallway or the parking lot and not even say hi.

That's changed. Meanwhile, Vermont's education campaign about floods and land use along the sides of rivers has gone out to the public through programs that are geared to as young as third and fourth graders, and also high schoolers, college students, and adults.

Those programs had already started before Tropical Storm Irene, but after the storm, said Todd Manees, a river management engineer for the state, "public awareness and concern about rivers and streams has heightened. It's now a stepped-up effort. Vermont is leading the nation."

ONE TOWN, ONE RIVER, TWO STORMS

All rivers have history, certainly those that flow through human settlement. The Chickley River in northwestern Massachusetts is one such river. It's not a big river, but it's big enough to have helped the community of Hawley develop as a prosperous mill town in the 1800s and it's also big enough to have felt the force of storms—both the natural and the human sort.

The Hurricane of 1938 that devastated much of New England, to take a memorable example, dumped twelve inches of rain on Hawley. Every bridge across the Chickley River and its tributaries was either swept away or knocked off kilter, roads were washed out, and countless homes were flooded.

Afterward townspeople came together, much as they had come together after the great flood of 1869 that wiped out local mills and bridges, and later the monster flood of 1927 that destroyed roads and property in town. Floods are part of life in hilly areas such as Hawley where rivers run through valleys, but some floods stand out for what they do to property and also for what they bring out in people.

The morning after the Hurricane of '38 a man in Hawley put out a call for volunteers to lay a temporary bridge across the Chickley River. Neighbors responded. As one local historian put it, "gradually the work of reconstruction went on until the task which had seemed insurmountable had been accomplished."[17] The full recovery of roads, bridges, and commerce in Hawley took years, supported in part by federal relief workers housed in a nearby town, but, at heart, it was community spirit that got Hawley back on its feet.

Seventy-three years after that experience Tropical Storm Irene pounded the town—the same storm that provided a lesson about wetlands upstream of Middlebury, Vermont. The roiling Chickley wiped out sections of a state road, washed the earth out from under a new public works garage, and damaged or swept away cabins, homes, and barns. Relief supplies for some isolated residents had to be airlifted in for a week.

But this storm didn't bring the community together as the Hurricane of '38 had. Irene ultimately pulled the town apart, and Hawley remained that way for quite some time.

There wasn't anything new in the floodwaters that caused this split. The difference resulted from different ideas about what should happen to a stream after floodwaters turn a river wild. One choice was to send in bulldozers to ream out the streambed, deepen its bottom, and armor its sides so to speed the flow of future floodwaters out of town. Alternatively, the town could repair the broken roads but leave it to the stream to adjust to the erosions and uprooting of trees and shifting of rocks that big storms can leave behind.

The decision in Hawley was to go with machines—magnificent excavators that dredged the Chickley River deep, smoothed out the bottom, pulled trees from the banks and lined the sides with crushed rock, leaving a five-mile-long channel with no greenery, no boulders, no rotting trees, or much else of the river's former self. Hawley wasn't the only town in the Northeast to order in the excavators, but the scope of the surgery there far surpassed that of any other place and led the Massachusetts state government to the remarkable decision a year later to order the town to undo much of what the earthmovers had done at its own cost.

The excavation of the Chickley River in Hawley was the idea of a local official. Shocked by the damage that the floods had done, Richard Desmarais, one of three elected selectmen in the town of 340 people, aimed to nail the problem of unruly water once and for all. He'd had no

---

17 Louise Hale Johnson, *The History of the Town of Hawley* (Mystic, CT: Charter Oak House, 1953), 136.

background in earthmoving or river science, but he'd watched a highway contractor rebuild a road that had been carved up by Irene's floodwaters. And he'd seen photos from the aftermath of the Hurricane of '38 that showed diesel-powered steam shovels in the river. The photos, supplied by the grandson of one of three local steam shovel operators who'd been pressed into river-repair service at the time, didn't show what the machines actually did in the river, but the impression on Selectman Desmarais was clear enough: here was muscle at work. By every account a take-charge fellow, Desmarais directed the highway contractor to put its machinery to work down a full five miles of the Chickley—dig it out, clean it up, line it with stone and leave it with banks high enough to contain any floodwaters that might come coursing through in the future. So it was that the Chickley River, a coldwater home to trout, a nursery for stocked salmon, a habitat for an endangered dragonfly, and an occasional venue for canoers and kayakers, was deepened, stripped of vegetation, and left as lifeless as a city gutter. In the vocabulary of river experts, the Chickley was channelized.

Desmarais, who died in late 2012 at age eighty, had history to go on. In addition to the photographic evidence of steam shovels, records in nearby towns mention earthwork following the Hurricane of '38 that included the excavation of river channels, the construction of heavy retaining walls, and the installation of levees made of rock and dirt.

But the context of 1938 was different from that of 2011. The intervening seventy-three years had brought new rules and laws that reflected fresh thinking about nature, among them the Massachusetts Conservation Commission Act (1955), the Massachusetts Wetlands Protection Act (1963), the formation of the state Department of Environmental Protection (1975), the passage of the Massachusetts Endangered Species Act (1990), and so on, plus simultaneously on university campuses the blossoming of studies in river science and the growth of businesses in the field of stream restoration. In the decades between 1938 and 2011, rivers and streams in Massachusetts picked up legal protections and a constituency of experts and advocates who could make noise.

Not long after excavators dug out the Chickley River, at some points leaving it ten feet deeper than it had been before the storm, an environmental group complained to the state government. The nonprofit

Connecticut River Conservancy, which is headquartered not far from Hawley, was started in 1952 mainly to protest sewage and industrial pollution of New England's longest river, but by 2011 its activities had extended to other concerns, including the protection of wetlands and streams throughout the region. In the case of the Chickley River, the conservancy alerted the state government to violations of environmental regulations the likes of which had never been seen.

The Commonwealth of Massachusetts came down hard on Hawley. State officials agreed that the storm had been a bad one, and in fact they'd given the town a temporary pass on wetlands rules for its most urgent repairs, but the stripping of five miles of the Chickley River went beyond the terms of that limited exemption. The channelizing of a wild river, the destruction of fish habitat, and violations of various state and federal environmental laws were such that the town and the highway construction company were ordered to undo what they had done at the cost of hundreds of thousands of dollars.

The order was celebrated by the river conservancy and some local residents, but it didn't go down well in every part of Hawley, a diffusely populated town where the river long ago ceased being a part of daily life for most people. In the early nineteenth century, when water-powered mills turned out broom handles, rakes, whip handles, and the like, Hawley was a different place, its population three times what it is now and its economy dependent on waterpower; in the late nineteenth century Hawley had a town square on a rise above the Chickley River that was surrounded by a church, a parsonage, a store, a post office, and a hotel, now all gone. It's a bedroom community today. Residents go to work and do their shopping elsewhere.

After the events of 2011 and 2012, the people of Hawley turned their attention inward; they flocked to town hall where they argued bitterly about whether the channelizing of the river was right or wrong and also about what had come of it—the probing by state officials, the settlement proceedings, the public ridicule, the fines, the government order to undo the fixes, the costs, the whole mess.

The tension between those who saw nothing wrong with reaming out the river and those who saw nothing right with it went deep, and it altered the very character and tone of conversation in the community. In most small New England towns these days, part-time and volunteer jobs in local government can go begging for candidates, and voter turnout is generally low at the once-a-year town meetings where citizens go back and forth over whether the old town dump truck can last another year, after which they generally move on. The Hawley town meeting in March 2013 was an exception. Nearly 75 percent of the town's voters turned out to pick a new selectman from a slate of three candidates. The town clerk read the results and then announced that she was resigning. "I don't think I have ever quit anything, but as of tonight it's different," she said. "I don't care to work with this new administration."[18] Within weeks, three other town officials resigned.

During the next several years, much of what had been done to the Chickley River after the storm was undone. The bottom of the dug-out river was raised, boulders were put back into the flow, logs and other parts of trees were pushed in, curves in the stream were engineered to create pools and pockets for aquatic life. In the spring of 2015, supported by funds from the river repair settlement, local volunteers and representatives from Americorps and Trout Unlimited planted 400 shrubs and trees along the river's banks, the purpose being to help prevent erosion and also provide cooling shade to aquatic life; in time, the plants and trees will shed leaves that, in decay, will join filmy algae on rocks in the river that will feed invertebrates at the bottom of the food chain; eventually new vegetation will take root on the banks, and downed trees in the water will rot; the river will become close to wild again.

It'll be decades before wildlife fully returns to the river, but that's far faster than had the Chickley been left flat as a highway and armored on the sides with stone riprap. A 1967 study in North Carolina reported that forty years after rivers there had been channelized, fish populations had only marginally recovered.[19]

As for the human community of Hawley, the recovery took time. Charles Stetson, among others, felt the tension acutely. A longtime resident who was Hawley's tax collector and treasurer at the time of the storm, he told me that the excavation was mischaracterized by the state and wrongly faulted. Further, he said, the initial reworking of the river made sense. "All

18 *The Recorder.* March 13, 2013.
19 Cited in Philip J. Soar and Colin R. Thorn, "Channel Restoration Design for Meandering Streams," (US Army Corps of Engineers, 2001), 43.

we did was take up debris so that the water could stay within its banks," he recalled, adding that the river handled the next big storm quite well. In his view, the redo of the original repair piled unneeded costs on taxpayers' shoulders. In 2013, Stetson ran for selectman in a three-man race and lost; he then moved out of town, as did some other residents who had argued the other side.

John Sears, the man who won that three-way election and who, early on, had criticized the channelizing of the Chickley, won a tight re-election race a year later. Asked late in 2015, more than four years after the flood, whether Hawley had recovered from the controversy, he answered without hesitation, "No."

Since those days many people in the area seem to have come around to the idea that confining rivers to rock-lined channels doesn't make sense; better to leave rivers free to overtop their banks from time to time so floodwaters can spread out and soak into unbuilt grounds where they lose their destructive energy. But the public's education in river science still has a way to go. That's based on a seemingly superficial thing, which is what they think a stream or a river should look like.

What about you? Picture a stream. Do you see a calming flow of water around rocks, framed by ferns, sublime and Eden-like—a page on a nature calendar? Or do you see a stream filled with the detritus of nature: rotting tree trunks cocked up on boulders, tangles of branches, the unruly crud of wilderness?

Most river science people go with the second picture, the mess. The downed wood provides homes to insects at the bottom of the food chain; tangled branches catch sediment that sustains aquatic life; crosswise logs create pools where baby fish get their start; in this picture rotting wood is a natural part of river systems.

Not everybody sees it that way, said John Gartner, a researcher at the University of Massachusetts in Amherst who's studied the Chickley River. Part of the restoration work there included dumping logs into the stream to replace ones that the original restorers had yanked out. On his field work Gartner met more than a few local people who allowed that they weren't too partial to debris in a stream; it upset their sense of order. Telling me this, he said with a tone of dismay, "There's this inherent desire to clean things out."

WHAT HAPPENS WHEN A STREAM MEETS A ROAD

The town where I live is so small that it has no stores, no streetlights, no stoplights, no crosswalks. Of the twelve miles of public roads in Roxbury, New Hampshire, population 211, more than half are dirt. Traffic control in town is limited to two stop signs.

There's one more thing, a seemingly inconsequential thing. At seventy-five different places along these roads, there are pipes that run beneath the surface from one side to the other.

These pipes, called culverts, drain roadside ditches in town and also carry the waters of intermittent and permanent streams. Their purpose is to reduce the chance of erosion and other water damage to roads and their surroundings. The culverts tend to get the job done, which helps explain why most people in Roxbury know little or nothing about them. No surprise. Until fairly recently, most towns and cities had no full record of where or how many culverts had been installed under streets and roads, nor what shape those culverts are in. That's changing as increasingly hard rains and the decay of old culverts are leading to costly washouts. Meanwhile, a whole new group of people have started paying attention to culverts, these being people whose concerns go to the welfare of fish and salamanders and other animals that can't get from one side of a road to the other due to the shape and condition of these pipes.

Both these groups—the people who are interested in the stability of roads and the people who are interested in the health of streams and what lives in them—want culverts to work right. The designs can be simple or complicated, but there's one elementary principle, always has been, which a professor at Union College in upstate New York put down in writing fully 165 years ago. Culverts, he wrote, "must be proportional to the greatest quantity of water which they can ever be required to pass." He added, thoughtfully, that the pipes "should be at least eighteen inches square, or large enough to admit a boy to enter to clean them out.[20]"

Modern design standards don't say anything about children being employed to clean out culverts, but the first condition—the one about handling the volume of water that's coming at them—has a particular

---

20 W. M. Gillespie, *A Manual of the Principles and Practice of Road-Making, Comprising the Location, Construction and Improvement of Roads and Rail-Roads* (New York: A. S. Barnes & Co., 1853), 178.

urgency in the Northeast today where, according to recent climate studies, precipitation from heavy storms has gone up more than in any other part of the country and is expected to get worse, and in the process invite damage, costs, and in some cases tragedy.

How odd that such lowly things should have such consequence! Yet, there they are at just about every place where a road crosses a stream or, put another away, at just about every place where a stream comes up against a road. Could there be any more literal intersection of human society and nature?

Among categories of infrastructure, culverts aren't anywhere near as distinctive as bridges and dams that span or block waters in full view of us all. But there's a lot more of them than dams and bridges combined, and therefore there's enough of them to show us a thing or two about humans' impact on nature—as the following two culverts showed me.

THE TRAGEDY OF WARREN BROOK

In October of 2005, a drenching rain fell on the small rural town of Alstead, New Hampshire, about ten miles from where I live—fifteen inches in twenty hours, enough to transform a little stream into a killer force.

Warren Brook, which on dry summer days can merely trickle, travels west to empty into the Connecticut River, and along the way it passes through a gorge in Alstead. For quite some time the gorge was spanned by a two-lane bridge that carried the traffic of Cooper Hill Road from one side to the other. In the 1960s the bridge needed repairs, and after some discussion it was decided that it would be cheaper to do away with the bridge and replace it with an earth embankment that had a culvert running through that would carry the waters of the brook on their westward course. The change was made. Shortly afterward, a spring flood damaged the culvert, so a larger and longer pipe was installed—this one wide enough to drive a pickup truck through and surely big enough to handle any floodwaters that would ever come its way.

So it was until the October rains of 2005. The culvert couldn't keep up with all the water that was filling the brook, including water from several beaver dams at higher elevations that had gotten washed out. The gorge behind the embankment began filling up, and an impromptu lake took shape. The water level in the impromptu lake climbed higher and higher, and ultimately reached the top of the embankment, which was more than forty feet above the bed of the stream, at which point the backed-up waters began eating away at the road.

At about seven in the morning of October 9, the road and the embankment beneath it gave way and sent a massive wall of water down the brook toward Alstead's downtown. The wave cleared away five miles of utility poles, knocked apart half a dozen bridges, carved roads into pieces, damaged or destroyed two dozen homes, filled farmland with mud, and drowned four people. When experts talk about unusual storms and weather events, they commonly use terms such as fifty-year floods or hundred-year storms. Sean Sweeney, a hydrologist who was involved with the recovery from this storm, described the Alstead flood to me as a 10,000-year event. "It was off the charts," he said.

Here's how one resident recalled it: "The noise was incredible: splintering, gushing water. The trees were actually being broken like toothpicks. Just take a sixteen- to eighteen-inch-diameter cane and break it over your knee; it's the sound of it. The ground was shaking." [21]

Today the embankment is no more. It wasn't replaced. Cooper Hill Road comes up to the edge of the gorge and ends there. Down below the brook flows on—unimpeded and as unconstrained as it had been before the culvert went in fifty years earlier.

The disaster in Alstead hasn't been matched anyplace else recently; 10,000-year floods don't come all that often. But worsening storms in recent years have set a lot of people thinking about whether the culverts that run beneath roads are big enough to handle the volumes of water that are coming at them. These include people who worry about public safety, and also people who worry about the costs of repair when culverts are overwhelmed with too much water or get clogged with sediment, wood, or ice and send waters rushing off to where they're not meant to go and cause costly rebuilding.

The worries stem from recent hard storms, particularly in the Northeast where rainfall from downpours is 70 percent heavier than it was a half-century ago[22] and many culverts are old, decrepit, and too small

---

21 Thomas W. Hancock, *Too Much Water Too Much Rain—The Story of the Alstead Flood*, Alstead Historical Society, ed. Cassandra Kreek, Emily K. Kreek, and Ian D. Relihan (Exeter, NH: Publishing Works, 2006), 42. Quoted by permission of the Alstead Historical Society.
22 National Climate Assessment, 2014.

to handle what's being demanded of them. The road agent in my town—he's the one-man department who plows in winter, paves in summer, and cleans out roadside ditches in the fall—has lately taken to replacing old drainage culverts with larger ones to make sure that stormwaters stay beneath roads and don't rise up to do damage that can be expensive to fix.

Replaced one at a time and mainly with ones that keep ditches dry, the replacements haven't cost taxpayers all that much. But in bigger places with bigger streams the costs of replacing a single culvert, particularly one that's already failed, can run very high.

The standard today, what with prospects of worsening storms is: bigger is better. It took time and expense and a lot of argument to get to this point, because until just a year ago the Federal Emergency Management Agency would give localities only enough disaster aid to replace busted culverts with ones the same size; if towns wanted larger replacements, that was on their dime. FEMA today helps pay for bigger replacements when the originals get wiped out, and in some cases won't put any money into same-size replacements. When it comes to dealing with failed culverts, one FEMA official told me, "Our goal is to fix it once."

The ideal, of course, is to not to have to fix anything at all. It costs more to repair damaged roads and rebuild stream crossings than to install new culverts on an orderly schedule. Plus, there are other costs that come with washouts, such as the costs to users of roads who have to be sent off on detours—truckers, commuters, and so on. One team of researchers found that the economic costs of those disruptions can far exceed the costs of culverts themselves.[23]

The researchers also raised an unsettling fact, which is that a great many of the big culverts that run beneath interstates, most of which were built in the 1960s through the 1980s, were designed to last thirty to fifty years; we're near or past the ends of some of those lifespans now, which suggests more problems and costs ahead.

THE COST OF A CULVERT

Ten years ago, a group of volunteers got together to count up all the stream crossings in the watershed of the Ashuelot River, a major tributary of the

---

23 Joseph Perrin Jr. and Chintan S. Jhaveri, "The Economic Costs of Culvert Failures," for the Transportation Research Board, 2004.

Connecticut River in southwestern New Hampshire. That river, which is sixty-four miles long, drains a rural watershed of 425 square miles that includes the lands around Roaring Brook. There'd been some flooding here and there, and there'd also been concerns about how some culverts were blocking the movements of wildlife, so why not get a full picture of the situation? The culvert-counters tallied up more than 800 of the things and then picked one of them—a six-foot-wide pipe that carried the waters of Falls Brook beneath Hale Hill Road in the town of Swanzey—for a major change.

There hadn't always been a culvert at the spot. A map from the late 1800s shows no crossing at all, but at a certain point a bridge over the brook was built, and the best guess is that the bridge was replaced with a pipe beneath the increasingly busy road sometime in the 1970s.

In 2016, the six-foot-wide pipe, fifty feet long, was replaced by an arched aluminum structure that spans the full twenty-three-foot width of the brook. The thing today looks more like a bridge than a traditional culvert. The brook now flows unimpeded and unconstrained in a rocky streambed beneath the road, its ten miles of trout habitat upstream now seamlessly connected to ten miles of habitat downstream—one continuous and unfragmented waterway that's pretty much how nature designed it. Today when rains fall hard, water doesn't get backed up behind the old pipe and shoot out the other end with fire-hose force; the stream crossing today doesn't alter the flow of water at all.

The price tag for the project was $250,000. That was more than ten times what the town's public works director told me it would have taken to simply replace the old culvert—not that he had had any intention of doing such a thing. To simply swap out a pipe the same size would have left the spot as exposed to stormwaters and flooding as it had been before.

As it turned out, local taxpayers paid only $15,000 cash for the job, plus $7,000 of services; the rest of the money came from state and federal agencies that, along with conservation groups led by Trout Unlimited, saw a chance to make a dramatic difference.

Not every culvert project runs a quarter-million dollars. And not every one of the hundreds of thousands of culverts in New England needs an upgrade. But more than a few will, thanks to age and the effects of harder storms. As to who'll pay the freight—whether for new crossings or to keep existing ones working—local taxpayers best get ready. There may be limits to how long outside agencies and environmental groups can shoulder the majority of costs.

The job begins with public education. That can be quite a job considering the subject. Rachelle Lyons, an assistant professor at Plymouth State University in New Hampshire who's studied where roads and streams meet, told me, "It is difficult to advocate for something that's not that glamorous."

Last time I looked, there was no National Culvert Awareness Day. Too wonky for you? It might be time for one.

Chapter 5

It Gets in the Water, Part I

How pollution happens—start counting the ways

≈ ≈ ≈ ≈

NOT JUST ONE THING GONE WRONG

On a day late in 1959 in Keene, New Hampshire, Timothy Hockett lifted a cup of water to his lips and took a drink. The six-year-old had been having a fine day, but soon he was feeling a bit queasy. Then real things began to happen. His temperature shot up. He vomited. His nose started to bleed. He wasn't ordinarily a sickly lad, but he was sick now, so his worried parents took him to the local hospital. The medical staff there had heard about intestinal problems going around, but Timothy appeared to have something different, so they admitted him for testing and observation.

Within days, fifteen other people with similar symptoms joined little Timothy in an isolated wing of the building; it turned out that they all had typhoid fever.

The disease, which involves severe intestinal inflammation, is highly infectious and can be fatal. But this was the second half of the twentieth century and this was the United States of America where ancient scourges such as typhoid and cholera and smallpox had been all but forgotten. It was a time and place of medical advance. Just the other day hadn't the local newspaper carried a story about how doctors in California for the first time had reattached the severed leg of a human? This was the age of public health and modern medicine and when, but for syphilis and the like, acute communicable disease was a thing of the American past.

A sanitary survey in Keene in 1934 had contained this comforting passage: "Typhoid fever is practically unknown so no measures are taken against it." A city health report fifteen years before that in 1919 listed only two cases of typhoid against eighty-one of scarlet fever, fifty-eight of mumps, thirty-six of measles, and 249 of influenza.

But here was typhoid on medical charts in a quarantined wing at Elliot Community Hospital, and little of it made sense. More than 20,000 people lived in the community, and apparently only sixteen of them had the disease. And those sixteen victims came from different neighborhoods, their families shopped at different markets, they got their milk from different sources, they had few if any social connections. They all got their water from the same city supply, but then why would only one member of any single household be infected?

Ultimately a local doctor did trace the typhoid to water. He followed a pipe to a reservoir in the neighboring town of Roxbury, and then went further up a brook to a still larger body of water—Woodward Pond. About 200 yards southeast of the upper reservoir he found a small encampment of loggers.

It was there, in a temporary shack that housed a woman and two woodcutters whom the city had been paying to clear trees, that authorities found their unsuspecting typhoid carrier, a man named John Bouchard.

Bouchard and his two companions had been careful about setting up a latrine for their wastes and the manure of their horses. But unusually heavy rains in late October overwhelmed their precautions without their knowing. The pile of wastes got so soaked that Bouchard's toxic organisms leaked into a small rivulet that trickled unseen around a bend and into Roaring Brook, and then on to the smaller downstream reservoir and into pipes that supplied water to the people of the city of Keene.

Odd. The city had taken precautions with its water. After a spate of gastroenteritis swept the community a quarter-century earlier, the authorities had installed a sand filter system. Ordinarily, the filters would have screened out the typhoid pathogens but, due to an unfortunate bit of timing, the disease got through to local taps.

Sand filter technology, which was in use all over the country, worked well but for the briefest period immediately following a cleaning. It happened that the torrential rains that washed the typhoid into Roaring Brook had arrived just after a servicing of the filters, underscoring the role of chance in the turns of history.

And so it was that the toxic molecules made their way into the public water system sufficiently diluted that only sixteen people caught the disease, and only one of them, an older man, died.

In Keene no one was prepared for the typhoid, certainly not the members of the city council who three years earlier had rejected a recommendation to chlorinate city water partly on the argument that people would complain about the taste.

City Hall now jumped to that treatment on an emergency basis, and, lacking insurance that would cover the contamination, turned to its lawyer to work out some quick settlements. Working behind the scenes, he negotiated deals with local lawyers and he separately briefed all fifteen city councilors at their homes, thereby avoiding a public discussion that would have drawn public attention to City Hall's prior rejection of chlorination and possibly send settlement costs through the roof.

Seven months after the typhoid incident, the Keene City Council approved $67,000 of settlements—roughly half a million dollars today. Out of the arrangement, young Timothy Hockett was awarded $2,331.33. Four decades later in an interview, he recalled that his nosebleeds continued for a dozen years until gradually going away. As to whether he retained any worries about the safety of local water, he replied, "No, not really."

That wasn't the case for another victim, Richard Bauries. Twenty-three at the time of his hospitalization, he lived the rest of his life until his death at age seventy-four in 2011 with an acute aversion to drinking water, according to his widow Pat. She added that he never forgot that during his thirty-four-day sequestration in the hospital he was fed on paper plates that were later burned. "Until the day he died, he could not eat off of paper plates," she recalled.

Richard Bauries lost his thick black hair in the experience; it grew back thin. He had to submit to Vitamin B inoculations for some years. But materially the consequences weren't all negative: The typhoid infection led to a $3,443.33 settlement that wound up being used as a deposit on the Bauries' first home.

Still, the experience was jarring. During his hospitalization, Richard Bauries shared a room with the only typhoid victim who died, an elderly man with serious pre-existing medical conditions. Recalled Pat Bauries: "He felt his mortality at that point."

Since those strange and frightening days, typhoid has never again gotten into a public water system in the United States. Thank better standards of hygiene, sanitation, and water treatment technology for that. Still, for all the science and money that have gone into wringing out—or keeping out—contaminants, a drink of water isn't guaranteed safe. Water may be life sustaining, yes, but it can also deliver harm under the wrong circumstances.

That's wrong circumstances, *plural*. As it was when typhoid found its way to household taps in Keene in 1959, contamination commonly comes from more than one thing going wrong—not just a pathogen on the loose but also perhaps a treatment plant that's not working particularly well on a certain day, or water works employees who aren't paying attention, or medical diagnoses that are off the mark, or even something new that might be going on inside humans themselves that exposes them to danger.

In 2008 and 2009, responding to a federal order to test their water, public works employees in Keene collected samples from their Roaring Brook supply and shipped them off to a government lab. The report came back that the water contained a parasite called cryptosporidium, source unknown.

The city's filtering system apparently trapped the parasite before it could make its way to local taps. Still, the city advised people who had weak immune systems to check with their doctors about whether to drink the water, and it kept reminding its customers of that concern for nearly a decade after the parasite had been detected.

The caution made sense, because the parasite was then and is now a reminder of the vulnerability of public water systems. It's also relatively new. Worries about cryptosporidium date to an event in 1987 in the foothills of the Appalachian Mountains in Georgia. As described in medical journals, heavy rains washed animal waste from a stockyard into a creek that emptied into the Little Tallapoosa River one mile upstream of the intake of the water treatment system of Carrollton, Georgia, population 25,000.

Within days, students at the University of Western Georgia in town began packing the infirmary with complaints of abdominal pains, vomiting, and diarrhea. The authorities first looked to the cafeteria for origins of the distress, but after complaints of intestinal problems began coming from other parts of town the problem was sourced to water. Eventually, 13,000 people were infected in the first recorded instance in the United States of cryptosporidium getting into a surface supply of drinking water.

The parasite had washed from the manure of infected cattle into a treatment system that at the time met federal and state requirements—on paper at least. But the system was being renovated and its filtering function was temporarily out of service. Phil C. Astin Jr., a physician who headed the local health department, recalled, "It was just bad luck that they were fooling around with the filters down there."[24]

In fact, cryptosporidium wasn't entirely new. Only its harm to humans was. The parasite was known a century ago but at the time only by veterinarians. Then in 1976, an otherwise healthy three-year-old girl in Tennessee was diagnosed with the condition. Half a dozen years later cryptosporidium was blamed for stomach problems for 200 people near San Antonio, Texas, after a leaking sewer pipe contaminated a public well. That's when water was found to be a carrier.

At about this time, cryptosporidium began appearing in scientific studies as an emerging and highly infectious threat to infants, frail elders and people with weak immune systems. Here, at last, was an explanation for mini-epidemics of watery diarrhea that had showed up around the country—at a day care center in New York, a swimming pool in Los Angeles, a campground in Pennsylvania, and elsewhere.

The cryptosporidium parasite isn't visible to the naked eye; its name variously translates from Latin as "underground spore" or "mystery spore." It has no scent. It has no color. It could be present in a reservoir or a stream or a glass of water or a bite of food and you wouldn't notice until it went to work on you. It's infinitesimal—a single-cell organism that can't be knocked out by the standard treatment of chlorine, the universal disinfectant. It is, in a word, amazing: A tiny organism wrapped in a durable outer shell that enables it to survive in a dormant state in nature for months, even years—a robust environmental vehicle, as scientists put it. Once inside a body, the cell finds the small intestine where digestive juices dissolve its outer shell at which point four protozoa emerge and begin to reproduce madly. The effect disrupts a body's ability to absorb water and nutrients, leading to dehydration; the body responds defensively by expelling the intruders through vomit and diarrhea, sending the parasite off to find new hosts—days later, months later, years later.

---

24 Darryl Enriquez, "Georgia Community Knows How Bad It Is to Lose Confidence in Tap Water," *Milwaukee Journal,* April 8, 1993.

For most healthy people infection means a couple of weeks of watery stools. But for people with weak immune systems, infections can spread throughout the intestinal tract and then to the gall bladder, the lungs, the pancreas. The effect, as an early report in the *New England Journal of Medicine* starkly put it, can be "unrelenting and fatal."[25]

In the early spring of 1993, cryptosporidium got into the water supply of Milwaukee, Wisconsin, and sickened 400,000 humans, killing more than seventy of them. The medical costs alone were in the tens of millions of dollars. It was the worst outbreak of any waterborne disease in the United States since record-keeping began in 1920.

The incident in Milwaukee was magnified by human error. Early on, local health authorities interpreted reports of sharply rising absenteeism from schools, hospitals, and factories as signs of a particularly bad flu going around, so they advised the public to drink lots of water. In time, labs turned up parasites in stool samples and a conclusion that cryptosporidium had gotten into the public water system from an intake pipe one mile out in Lake Michigan.

In the detective work that followed, the source was variously determined to be cattle that were being kept near rivers that flowed into Lake Michigan, or leakage of toxins from slaughterhouses, or unobserved recycling of infected human sewage into the drinking water system following a period of heavy rain. Whatever the origin, filters at one of Milwaukee's water treatment plants were dirty, hence ineffective, and workers at the plant failed to pick up on the contamination because a monitoring system there had been installed incorrectly and was out of use.[26]

Sickness swept the city and rippled outward. Crew members on a Coast Guard cutter that had filled its tanks in Milwaukee at the time of the contamination and that was now out at sea began showing symptoms of illness. Hockey fans who'd attended a national college tournament in town took the illness back home, some as far away as Maine. The crisis in Milwaukee ended only after a boil water order went out.

A year later, a cryptosporidium outbreak took forty-three more lives

25 William R. MacKenzie et al, "A Massive Outbreak in Milwaukee of Cryptosporidium Infection Transmitted through the Public Water Supply," *New England Journal of Medicine* 331, no. 3 (1994): 161.
26 Kate Foss-Mollan, *Hard Water: Politics and Water Supply in Milwaukee, 1870–1995* (Purdue, IN: Purdue University Press, 2011).

in Las Vegas, Nevada. The source was never confirmed, but drinking water from Lake Mead was tagged as the likeliest suspect.

The contaminations in Milwaukee and Las Vegas received wide attention not only for the distress that they caused but also for their place in another emerging health dilemma at the time: most of the victims who died had had HIV or AIDS, meaning that their immune systems weren't strong enough to protect against an illness for which there was, and still is, no biological defense except a healthy immune system.

Shortly after these events, officials in Washington launched a study of cryptosporidium, returning to a job that they'd shelved years earlier so that they could focus their research on pollution from synthetic chemicals.[27]

Ultimately the experts concluded that human vulnerability to cryptosporidium was very real and that the parasite couldn't be knocked out by chlorine. That finding led to billions of dollars of spending on filtering equipment in water treatment plants across the country.

The plant that processes the waters that come out of Roaring Brook was outfitted with such a filtering system, and the system apparently has done its job so far as cryptosporidium's concerned. But worries about the parasite remain, in part, because the segment of the population that's most at risk is on the rise, that being people with weak immune systems. Each year in the United States, 29,000 people receive organ transplants, 48,000 others are newly diagnosed with HIV, 28,000 others learn they have AIDS, and more than 1.5 million others begin chemotherapy for cancer. None of these population groups existed before the second half of the twentieth century, when some modern diseases and modern medicines began reducing immune systems to rubble.

What does it take, then, to guarantee a safe drink from waters that arrive through pristine settings such as those of Roaring Brook? Beyond money and technology, it takes a suspension of belief that science and regulation can fully guarantee a safe drink. To be sure, a lot's been accomplished; you won't find typhoid pouring out of faucets in rural New England any more, for example. But cryptosporidium remains a mystery. Since 1988, the Water Research Foundation in Denver, Colorado, has

---

27 *Safe Drinking Water Act Amendments of 1995: Hearing before the Committee on Environment and Public Works, United States Senate*, 104th Congress, first session, (October 19, 1995). (Testimony by Richard James Bull on *S. 1316, a bill to reauthorize and amend Title XIV of the Public Health Service Act (commonly known as the "Safe Drinking Water Act"), and for other purposes)*, at 65.

spent more than $40 million on nearly one hundred research projects on the subject, and it's still at the job; type in "cryptosporidium research" on the Internet and settle in for a long afternoon.

Or for a distraction you might go looking for a video game that Pandemic Studios, a California firm, came out with in 2005. The game's based on an alien character named Cryptosporidium-137 who arrives on the planet to do significant mischief. The name of the game: "Destroy All Humans!"

THE WONDERS AND HAZARDS OF MODERN CHEMISTRY

Roaring Brook is not every stream. It's remote and surrounded by trees, the only unforested parts being the surfaces of the two reservoirs that it connects. You won't find any apartment complexes on its shores nor stores, factories, paved roads, or farms. In ecological terms, the stream is protected. This condition owes to land conservation around the stream and its reservoirs over the years, and also largely to an unplanned turn of events more than a century ago that's known to historians as The Abandonment.

During the second half of the nineteenth century, the population in the hilly interiors of northern New England went into sharp decline as large mills in big cities lured away country folk for steady wages, the laying of railroad tracks to the fertile plains of the Midwest took populations to greener pastures, and then the Civil War wiped out men who, had they survived, would have put their lands to productive use and kept the community growing.

In the town of Roxbury where Roaring Brook flows, the first federal census in 1820 recorded 366 residents. By 1880, the population was down to 126. By the time of Roxbury's centennial in 1912, the total number of voters in town—all male—was 12. In time, the popularization of cars helped usher in the concept of bedroom communities and suburbs, and the population of the town began growing back. The census today is 211, still well below what it was nearly two centuries ago. Like a fair number of other town residents today, I can't see another house from where I live.

One theory about The Abandonment is that the decline of population resulted not only from external influences—railroads, jobs elsewhere, a devastating war—but also from what people in the hills brought on themselves. By this I mean the wholesale stripping of land for wood and pasture, which led to erosion that washed nutrients out of already poor soils, leaving farmers with harvests too small to count for much of anything and reason enough to go looking elsewhere to make a life.[28] This is the ecological take on The Abandonment that, so far as the health of Roaring Brook is concerned, had an unexpectedly good end.

The Abandonment caused the hill country to miss out on the march of modernity that altered the landscapes of so many other places. For close to half a century, the area stood forgotten—depopulated, out of sight and of no interest to anyone but animals in the wild, humans who hunted them and a few owners of summer homes. In 1958, when the city of Keene last bought land around Roaring Brook for the purposes of protecting its drinking water supply, it acquired 452 acres in ten different tracts. There was no prior development on those parcels—no shops, no apartment buildings with parking lots, no paved roads, no businesses and no houses with septic tanks leaking into the ground.

By sleeping through much of the twentieth century, then, the lands around Roaring Brook missed the boat on progress as the term is variously defined. Progress such as Tide.

In the 1940s, concluding more than a decade of research into what was secretly termed "Product X," Procter & Gamble came out with a synthetic substitute for the natural fats and oils that traditionally went into laundry soaps. The product, filled with chemical brighteners, softeners, fragrances, enzymes, stabilizers, wetting agents, salts, and so on, did a better job of cleaning than the old ways did, and it left clothes feeling softer, too. In short order, competitors came out with their own artificial soaps, each of them using phosphates, which to chemists are compounds of phosphorous bonded to oxygen, and which to Proctor & Gamble's marketing team formed the basis for claims that Tide was a "washday miracle." Phosphates lifted dirt off clothes and kept it off during the washing cycle.

Consumers were happy, but there were consequences—not that Roaring Brook and the lands immediately around it had any direct experience, the town being so lightly populated. What follows, then is an

28 Peter Thorbahn and Stephen Mrozowski, "Ecological Dynamics and Rural New England Historical Sites" in Anthropology Department Research Reports series, *Research Report 18: Ecological Anthropology of the Middle Connecticut River Valley.* Paper 10, 1979.

alternative history speculation about what could have happened to the waters of Roaring Brook had the area not been forgotten and left rural and, in fact, had gone the other way.

Picture it, apartments each equipped with a washing machine that emptied into septic systems that at some point or another could have sprung a leak, as happens. The escaping fluid would have oozed downhill in a subsurface plume. Along the way some of the nutrients from the liquid would have been drawn up into the roots of little rushes and sedges and other plants, perhaps mixing with other chemical residues from fertilizers that could also have been used to green up the lawns around the apartments. The rest of those nutrients would have wound up in the stream and its reservoirs where they would have been taken up as food by algae.

Algae are plants that don't look like plants. They lack flowers, roots, and leaves; their appearance can be bluish or greenish in color and their texture can appear as scum. With temperatures warm enough and daylight long enough and the supply of nutrients heavy enough, the algae in the reservoirs would have eventually become quite thick and quite broad—sucking up all the oxygen in the water, the effect being to leave the surface of the water a smooth film interrupted only by reflections off the bellies of fish that had been deprived of air and suffocated.

The tendency of algae to make such things happen in water was little noticed until the second half of the twentieth century when residues of detergents and chemical fertilizers began showing up in waterways, causing lakes to change color and sometimes turn toxic. The algae began clogging water treatment systems, which made those systems more expensive to operate; the algae caused lakes to stink like rotten eggs and leave itchy rashes on swimmers' skins and cause discomfort in their bellies. In 1999 health authorities in Vermont reported that two dogs that drank untreated algae-loaded waters from Lake Champlain died. Scientists have since detected possible ties between blue-green algae and the development of neurological conditions such as Lou Gehrig's disease.[29]

In August 1964, researchers reported with alarm that a 2,600-square-mile section of the bottom of the Lake Erie was without any oxygen at all—the area, equivalent to more than twice the size of the state of Delaware, was said to be dead—and much of the blame was laid on

---

29 Lindsay Konkel, "Are Algae Blooms Linked to Lou Gehrig's Disease?" in Environmental Health News, *Scientific American* (December 11, 2004).

detergent phosphates that had gotten through sewage treatment systems and into the water. Across the country, state legislatures, alarmed by smaller but similar crises, began debating whether to order the removal of phosphates from detergents.

The debate brought out the rhetoric. Jesse Steinfeld, the surgeon general of the United States who had campaigned against such ills as tobacco, DDT, and the artificial sweetener cyclamate—by that record, an enlightened man—took quite a different stance on phosphates. "In an emotional atmosphere of excessive and unproved statements," he wrote, "the nation recently got caught up in a controversy over clothes-washing that has become a classic case of environmental extremism and governmental ineptitude."[30]

Steinfeld also argued that some proposed substitutes for phosphates could cause birth defects and even cancer. He insisted, "I don't want to be Surgeon General while doing a carcinogenesis experiment on 200 million people."[31]

But water-purity people kept campaigning, and in 1993 the major players in the $4 billion laundry detergent market pledged to strip out the phosphates. Fifteen years later state regulators turned their attention to dishwasher detergents that contained phosphates; in 2014, nearly seventy years after Procter & Gamble first came out with its phosphate-infused "washday miracle," the consumer products company announced that it would remove the ingredient from all its products worldwide.

So ended the detergent problem. But modern chemistry has produced still other miracles that have altered the water in lakes and streams. By this I mean the residues from sunscreens, aerosols, perfumes, food supplements, bug sprays, and pet medicines, as well as the mood enhancers, the hormone boosters, the oral contraceptives, the antibiotics, the painkillers, many of which manage to make it through wastewater treatment systems entirely intact and float downstream, perhaps to a swimming area, perhaps to the intake pipe for a drinking water system.

Only an imaginative and remarkably adventurous society could produce such conveniences and medical wonders for its people, assisted by a lack of curiosity and a careless attitude. Shockingly little is known

---

30 *Reader's Digest.* November 1973, 2 and 6.
31 Simon Dresner, "The detergent mess . . . What to tell your wife," *Popular Science* (January 1972), 16.

about what can come of these synthetic wonders. Alarms are being raised today, and they have been raised in the past; here's one such caution from a symposium on water pollution in 1960, well before most Americans gave a thought to what they were letting into the water:

> "Today man is faced with many new and exotic chemicals of complex organic composition which are being used as cleansing agents, pesticides, insecticides, weedicides and fertilizers. Very little is known concerning the long-term buildup of these chemicals or the effects. Certainly the use of such complex chemicals should be limited to areas some distance removed from water courses or impoundments."[32]

In 1907, the Ohio-based Chemical Abstracts Service, a subsidiary of the American Chemical Society, began compiling a registry of chemical substances, and by the 1970s its managers felt that they knew enough about the subject to declare that there was a predictable limit. They theorized that the number of man-made chemicals and compounds would eventually top out at seven million.

Twenty years later the agency reported the creation of the fifty millionth compound—a molecule called Arylmethylidene heterocycle (the formal designation is $(5Z)$-5-[(5-Fluoro-2-hydroxyphenyl) methylene]-2-(4-methyl-1-piperazinyl)-4$(5H)$-thiazolone) that was developed to help reduce neuropathic pain.

All this paints a terrifically unsettling picture: 50 million chemical compounds, most of them unregulated, finding their ways into rivers and lakes that supply household water for people to drink. It's almost enough to swear off public water that comes from reservoirs and instead sink a private well.

If that alternative has any appeal, I suggest a visit to the first floor of City Hall in Keene, New Hampshire. Through the doors of the modest brick building and past the revenue collection office on the right, you'll notice near the elevator a colorful wall display with a sign on top that says "Our Groundwater." The display is an artist's rendition of a rural landscape

---

32 E. J. Allen, "Water Supply Watershed Problems—Seattle Watershed" in *Proceedings of the Seventh Symposium on Water Pollution Research*, US Department of Health, Education & Welfare, Public Health Service, Region IX (Portland, OR, April 1960), 16.

with a couple of farms and houses and a few shops and roads and other markers of civilization. There's a well at the bottom of the display that goes deep into the ground. Underneath all this are six buttons that are marked with little signs: "Septic Systems," "Landfills," "Antifreeze and motor oil," and so on. Push one of the buttons—say, the one that's marked "Golf Courses"—and immediately a line of little lights goes on showing how herbicides and pesticides that are used on golf courses wind up leaching into the ground and eventually winding up in wells.

The display was made by a local man on a federal grant in 1997 to alert the public to how pollution can get into ground water. The display was part of a traveling exhibit to local schools and community groups, and when the grant ran out, the display was given a home in Keene's City Hall. Twenty years on, the device still works, a credit to the maker. Jim Gruber, an environmental science professor at Antioch Graduate School in Keene who had a hand in the original project, said, "It helped connect the dots."

In those terms, there are plenty of dots to connect—even more than those that appear on the display today. They include new chemical formulations and also naturally formed substances that wind up in groundwater and wells. For example:

- Gasoline additives: In the 1990s, responding to tough new federal air-quality rules, gasoline refiners in the United States increased their use of the smog-reducing additive Methyl Tertiary Butyl Ether that's popularly known as MTBE. Not long afterward homeowners with wells near gas stations noticed unpleasant odors and tastes in their water, and they complained of nausea and dizziness. The problems were traced to MTBE. In 2005 refiners quit using the additive but the effects of the contamination remained: In New Hampshire, hundreds of private wells were polluted by the chemical. The state sued refiners and other gasoline suppliers, saying they knew that the chemical could pollute groundwater. All but ExxonMobil reached a settlement before trial that sent $90 million into digging up old storage tanks, removing contaminated dirt, and laying water lines to affected properties. ExxonMobil took its chances with a jury and lost. The company was ordered to cough up $236 million to help pay for cleanup.

- Plastics: In the early 1950s, DuPont Chemical Company began using a new chemical for a wondrous consumer innovation: nonstick cookware. The compound, Perfluorooctanoic acid, was later linked to various cancers, thyroid disease, and colitis among other conditions. In 2016, traces of PFOA began showing up in well water in New Hampshire near several plastics plants. The state government began shipping bottled water to a couple of hundred families, and the federal Environmental Protection Agency began calling the chemical an "emerging contaminant."
- Arsenic: In 2015, New Hampshire officials reported that more than 40,000 people who get their water from private wells were consuming excessive amounts of arsenic, a carcinogen that forms naturally in bedrock.[33] A study commissioned by the Centers for Disease Control and Prevention estimated that as many as 600 cases of lung, bladder, or skin cancer in the state could be avoided annually if arsenic-laced well water were properly treated.
- Lead: In 2016, the United States Geological Survey reported that ground water in eleven states, including every state in New England but Vermont, was corrosive enough to leach lead and other hazards from old plumbing into water that comes out of private wells.[34] This was quite apart from the situation in Flint, Michigan, where in 2014 corrosive water was sent into pipes that leached lead into what came out of local taps.

This chapter (and the following one) is about what can wind up in water that we drink. It's not a particularly pretty picture, despite statistics that suggest otherwise. There are 155,000 public water systems in the United States and 15 million private wells. In an ordinary year, fewer than 1,500 Americans report that they get sick from drinking contaminated water.[35] In a nation of 320 million people, that's a credit to technology, training, and standards of public health.

33 Mark Borsuk, Kathrin Lawlor, Laurie Rardin, Thomas Hampton, and Community Health Institute, "Arsenic in Private Wells in New Hampshire Year 2 Final Report," (Hanover, NH: Dartmouth Toxic Metals Superfund Research Program, Thayer School of Engineering at Dartmouth, 2015).

34 Kenneth Belitz, Bryant C. Jurgens and Tyler D. Johnson, *Potential corrosivity of untreated groundwater in the United States—Scientific Investigations Report 2016-5092.* USGS, 2016.

35 "Foodborne and Waterborne Disease Outbreaks—United States 1971–2012," Division of Foodborne, Waterborne, and Environmental Diseases, National Center for Emerging and Zoonotic Infectious Diseases, CDC, 2015.

Then again, the numbers don't include the untold numbers of Americans who've been merely alarmed or otherwise grossed out by what's in the water in their wells. They include, to pick a particularly revolting example, homeowners near a parcel of land in Hanover, New Hampshire, where animal carcasses from Dartmouth Medical School labs were buried decades earlier, wrapped only in plastic as was legal at the time; water well tests recently turned up signs of the radioactive compound—a carcinogen—that had been used in the medical school research.

These and other discoveries help explain why Americans spend hundreds of millions of their own dollars each year purifying and filtering water that comes out of their faucets at home, and also why Americans consume an astonishing thirty-four gallons of bottled water per capita each year. In sum, an awful lot of bad stuff gets into the water that we drink, in more than a few cases from truly wondrous innovations that seemed perfectly harmless when they came into our lives.

A PIPE STORY

Depending on the season and local rainfall, most of the water that flows down Roaring Brook winds up entering a pipe that takes it down into a valley and then up over a hill to a treatment plant, and from there the water heads into 112 miles of subterranean water mains and service lines to homes and businesses in the city of Keene and its surroundings. The distribution system is standard for cities, nothing unusual about it.

Most people don't generally think much about water pipes, whether in Keene or anywhere else, mainly because they're out of sight. Plus, pipes do their assigned jobs remarkably well.

But our confidence in water pipes—whether they're made of hollowed out logs or, in later years, cement, iron, steel, lead, and plastic—isn't always justified.

For one, pipes can leak, certainly older ones. By one measure, as many as six billion gallons of drinking water are lost through leaking pipes in the United States every day, and that's after cities and towns have spent countless millions of dollars of taxpayers' and ratepayers' money to protect, collect, and treat the water that's running through them. The Environmental Protection Agency puts the annual loss to utilities at $2.6

billion. Estimates of what it would take to patch up or replace those pipes run to half a trillion dollars—a proposition that in the halls of government presents a predictable answer to the question do you spend money fixing up pipes that are doing an okay job or, alternatively, do you spend the money on projects that voters can see with their own eyes such as street upgrades with nice new sidewalks and lighting?

There are a couple of other things to know about water pipes in addition to their capacity to leak, including what goes on inside them. You might imagine their insides being antiseptic, as clean as a soda fountain straw, but things can go on in there that aren't all that comforting to know. Ask the residents of Flint, Michigan. In the spring of 2014, local officials switched their source of drinking water from Lake Huron, a longtime supply, to a river that had particularly corrosive water. Not long afterward, local doctors began reporting heightened lead levels in blood tests of children. It was soon confirmed that the water, which the city had decided not to treat for its unusual hardness—in violation of federal law—was pulling lead out of the city's waterlines and ultimately exposing thousands of children to lifetimes of learning disability and hyperactivity, among other conditions.

Lead poisoning isn't the only thing that can get started inside water pipes. Chlorine, the universal disinfectant that revolutionized the delivery of drinking water a century ago, can cause problems, too. In the early 1970s, a chemist working for the Rotterdam water supply in Holland found that when chlorine came into contact with naturally forming organic material inside pipes—the microbial residues of decomposing leaves, for example—it produced byproducts that are unsafe for human health. Later research found chlorine inside water pipes can produce hundreds of byproducts, some of which have been linked to bladder cancer and low birth weights and many of which haven't been studied in depth. About twenty years ago, some water utilities began trying out a substitute called chloramine, a compound made from chorine and ammonia gas, that wound up getting even worse reviews.

Holland doesn't use chlorine to disinfect its water anymore; instead it aggressively agitates and filters its water before sending it on to customers. The city of Keene, for its part, has been adding chlorine to its Roaring Brook supply ever since its troubling experience with typhoid in 1959, apparently to good effect, but twice since 2003 tests have turned up unsafe chlorine byproducts; the city responded by altering the disinfectant mix and alerting the public. Then, too, there are the complaints about taste and smell and color from customers who, depending on where they live along a distribution network, don't all get the same concentration of chlorine in their water.

This is to say that the quality of our drinking water is a product of not one thing but many—the condition of the raw water, the disinfection, and then the possible chemical interactions than can happen inside the pipes, and so on. There's one more thing, a curious one, having to do less with water itself than the way in which water actually moves when it's inside pipes.

Out in the wild, the water in any brook or stream is moved along by simple gravity as it flows downhill, bouncing off rocks and around fallen trees. But once the water is inside the pipes of a water distribution system its motion is determined not so much by gravity but by pressure, and that can have consequences.

Here's a particularly dramatic example. The setting is Worcester, a city of 180,000 people in south-central Massachusetts. The year is 1969. The contamination is hepatitis.

In late August of that year, firefighters in Worcester responded to a two-alarm fire in a tenement building. They tapped into two hydrants that were connected to a municipal network of pipes that also served the practice fields of the Holy Cross College football team two miles away.

The practice fields' neighborhood included a condemned building where an adult and four children had been living. The summer had been dry and hot, and the children had taken to playing in water that they'd managed to get out of one of the outlets of the football field irrigation network; apparently while playing the children had taken to defecating on the ground. One final point: the city of Worcester was then facing an upsurge in infectious hepatitis, which at the time was believed to be the only viral disease that could be transmitted by water.

The water pressure at the football fields was already quite low, owing to a waterline break elsewhere in the system. Therefore, when the firemen pulled water out of the hydrants even two miles away, that caused the pressure in the pipes at the practice field to fall so low that the pressure actually reversed itself. That meant that the water that was sitting outside the pipes was sucked back into the irrigation system, taking with it any contamination that it encountered along the way.

The day before the fire in the tenement building, the Holy Cross varsity football team had reported to campus for early training. On the second day of practice, hours after city firemen had inadvertently caused hepatitis-tinged water to be sucked into the field irrigation pipes, members of the team drank heavily from a faucet that was at the end the irrigation network.

Four weeks of incubation later, football season started and things didn't go well for the Holy Cross Crusaders. They felt listless during their first game in a 13–0 loss to Harvard, and the following week the team took less than a full squad to Dartmouth, where during the game some players had to be helped off the field in a 38–6 loss.

In short order, Type A hepatitis was diagnosed, players were quarantined, and the rest of the season was canceled. To help make up for the loss of ticket sales, Dartmouth proposed that other colleges make donations to Holy Cross—$35,000 was raised. And, in a turn of events that reflected the national reach of the story, the Sacramento State College football team in California dedicated its season to Holy Cross; in their final game of the year against the University of Puget Sound-Sacramento players wore the Holy Cross Crusaders' purple and white jerseys. The Holy Cross co-captains were flown out to see the game, which Sacramento won 49–24. "That game was our gift from the California boys," recalled one of the co-captains.

The acts of generosity and empathy brought a warming end to what came to be known as the "Missing Season" at Holy Cross. The larger story is less comforting, which is that what happened on a college practice field in Worcester, Massachusetts—a phenomenon that's known as backflow, in which pressure within a water system reverses itself—is common enough to support the existence of a national trade association, the American Backflow Prevention Association in West Hartford, Connecticut, that has annual conventions and trade shows around the country, and that even puts out a comic book featuring a bright-eyed problem-solver who goes by the name Buster Backflow.

The phenomenon worries a lot of people for good reason. Consider this literally explosive case in 1982 in Connecticut when workers set out to repair a propane storage tank. As a preliminary step, they arranged to flush out the tank with water from a nearby fire hydrant. They connected one end of a hose to the hydrant and the other end to the tank, unaware that the internal pressure of the propane tank was greater than the water pressure at the hydrant. Once the hose was connected, the gas in the tank rushed into the hose, pushing the lower-pressure water before it and causing the water to flow back into the hydrant and then beyond into the pipes of the public water system in the community, with the gas following close behind. Within minutes residents in the area noticed hissing noises coming out of their sinks and toilets. In one house, a washing machine exploded; two houses caught fire.[36]

There are devices that can prevent such things from happening, and most American building codes today have a chapter about them. Still, apparently, there remains much to know. The Backflow Prevention Association's recent conferences have included presentations about recent cases of contamination and talks about other backflow possibilities, including, ominously, a session run by officials from the Department of Homeland Security whose principal concern is terrorism.

Bottom line: Water, once it's taken in from the wild and sent into pipes, doesn't enter an immaculate and protected zone. It merely enters a new place where new things can happen before it reaches the tap at home, the water fountain at the mall or some other place where you just might like a sip of water.

---

36 TREEO Center, University of Florida: https://treeo.ufl.edu/backflow/epa-resources/back-flow-case-histories/#k

Chapter 6

It Gets in the Water, Part II

Intention, inattention, and what can happen next

≈ ≈ ≈ ≈

WATCHING OUT FOR WATER TERRORISM

For a man who's over ninety, Bill Hooper is quite the active fellow. On summer days if he's not out mowing his lawns he's at the controls of a large backhoe somewhere on his forested property doing who knows what. He's young in spirit and he's a good talker, and when he gets talking about the past he can take you back to the moment.

One of his stories is from a summer's evening in 1943 when he was fifteen. He and a friend carried their fishing rods along a dirt road around the north side of Babbidge Reservoir in Roxbury, and after they crossed Roaring Brook they set up a camp to fish for hornpout. Hornpout, a species of catfish, bite at night, and in darkness Hooper and his pal were hauling 'em in when they noticed car lights on the other side of the reservoir. An odd thing, a car at night on the service road to the reservoir, driving up and coming to halt. Hooper and his friend paid close attention after they faintly made out three or four people getting out of the car. They heard voices coming across the water, and then a sentence that more than seventy years later Hooper remembers with distinct clarity, the words being: "This looks like a good place to dump the stuff."

The juices of patriotic service kicked in. This was a time when ordinary citizens dutifully scanned the skies for enemy planes and reminded homeowners to keep their window shades down at night. Even children knew to be on the alert, and Bill Hooper was one of them.

Hooper and his friend were off on a run, dashing a half-mile through the forest in the dark of night to the home of Harry Menter, the constable in the little town of Roxbury—right into the house ("People didn't lock their doors in those days," Hooper recalled) to wake up the constable and breathlessly tell him about something unusual and possibly dangerous going on up at the reservoir. The constable dressed and got into his car and, accompanied by the two boys, took the service road to the spot where they had seen the car. After some looking they found the vehicle, now off to the side and partly hidden at a dead-end in the woods.

At this point, the occupants of the car presented themselves, and wasn't it a surprise that they were all teenagers themselves not much older than Hooper himself, and in fact one of them was the constable's own son, and wasn't that cause for a big laugh?

"They'd been out looking for something to do," recalled Hooper. "In those days you didn't knock down or break stuff. You just did other stuff."

The stuff in this case was an occasion for merriment, fooling a couple of kids into thinking the war had come to town. Even constable Menter got a chuckle out of it. Word got out. "We were the laughing stock of the town, going down and waking up Harry Menter. Everybody was laughing but me," recalled Hooper, who conceded that if he had been a few years older at the time he just might have been on the other side of the joke.

As for the basis of the joke—that an enemy operative would think to penetrate the interior of northern New England to poison the water supply of a small rural city—that seems a stretch, but who can ever be too sure?

In 1917, the year the United States entered World War I, Keene's City Hall deployed guards to watch over Woodward Pond, then the only reservoir that supplied water from Roaring Brook.

Records in 1942, not long after the country entered World War II, show an outlay of $5,900 for special monitoring of the city's water supply including the stream.

In 1941, following the Japanese bombing of Pearl Harbor, Federal Bureau of Investigation Director J. Edgar Hoover publicly warned: "It has long been recognized that among public utilities water supply facilities offer a particularly vulnerable point of attack to the foreign agent, due to the strategic position they occupy in keeping the wheels of industry turning and in preserving the health and morale of the American populace."[37]

The sense of caution has never entirely gone away. Within minutes of the terrorist attacks on September 11, 2001, to take a recent example,

---

37 Claudia Copeland and Betsy Cody, "Terrorism and Security Issues Facing the Water Infrastructure Sector." Resources, Science, and Industry Division, Congressional Research Service, May 2003.

authorities in New York City did what you might expect: they closed bridges and tunnels to Manhattan, they diverted flights from local airports, they evacuated the United Nations headquarters, and so on. Some steps, however, were less obvious than others. At 10:30 a.m., ninety minutes after the second plane hit, Joel A. Miele Sr., the commissioner of New York's Department of Environmental Protection, issued an order that barred all recreational activity on the lands that surrounded the city's drinking water reservoirs, some of them more than one hundred miles away: "(F)ishing and hiking privileges are suspended until further notice. Unusual incidents or activities in the watershed may be reported to . . ."

Here was a vulnerability that few of the nine million consumers of New York's water had probably ever given much thought to. Eventually, worries about sabotage of drinking water reached well beyond New York as Washington ordered the operators of the 8,000 largest water works in the nation to examine their exposure to biological, chemical and physical attack.

Officials in Keene were among the 8,000. They went looking to the watershed and waters of Roaring Brook and also the network of subterranean pipes that deliver those waters to homes, businesses, and schools. They then drafted a surveillance and readiness strategy without a word of public discussion, lest any outsider learn too much.

For all the shock and surprise that came with the 9/11 attacks, the vulnerability of water had been anticipated. Three years earlier in May 1998, President Bill Clinton signed Presidential Decision Directive 63 that among other things ordered federal agencies to start talking with state and local governments about protecting roads, bridges, and water from terrorist assault.

Intentional fouling of public water wasn't out of the question, after all. In 1999 during the hostilities in Kosovo, cadavers wound up floating in wells. Far deeper in history, some aqueducts of the Roman Empire were engineered through tunnels specifically to avoid contamination or interruption by enemy forces.

Early in 2001, months before 9/11, the FBI came upon plans by what it termed a "very credible, well-funded North Africa-based terrorist group" to damage major water supplies in the United States. The threat was later found to be a hoax, but in the years that followed the government turned up more plausible threats, including the discovery of al-Qaeda maps of several drinking water systems, and also evidence of tampering with dams. In 2013, an Iranian man allegedly accessed the computerized control system of a small flood control dam in a community just north of New York City that had a history of costly floods; he failed to cause any damage because, in a lucky turn, the dam's sluice gate had been manually disconnected for maintenance.

The prospect of water terrorism, as it's now called, isn't only of foreign origin. In 1972, members of a white American supremacist group called the Order of the Rising Sun were arrested in Chicago for planning to dump seventy pounds of typhoid culture into the water supplies of several large United States cities that had what they considered to be "inferior" populations.[38] In 1985, a survivalist organization in Arkansas named The Covenant, The Sword, and The Arm of the Lord was caught planning to pour thirty gallons of potassium cyanide into the reservoirs of several big cities, the goal being to hasten the return of the Messiah by wiping out unrepentant sinners. As to the logistics of the enterprise—experts later said that it would take as many as ten tons of cyanide to effectively poison a single big-city reservoir—one of the conspirators was reported to say that God would have taken care of the dilution problem.[39]

But even granting the helping hand of God, reservoirs generally don't make a viable target. If you were to look upon the waters of Roaring Brook or any other stream feeding a drinking water reservoir, millions of gallons, even billions of gallons flowing in and out, you'd see soon enough that it would take an awful lot of poison to make a difference.

One authority on this subject was Abbie Hoffman, not a widely credentialed authority on hydrology to be sure, but still a man who appeared to have grasped the math of dilution. Hoffman, a cofounder of the Youth International Party known as the Yippies that protested the Vietnam War among other perceived wrongs, offered his views about water contamination in court testimony in 1969. A defendant in the trial of the Chicago Seven, a group of demonstrators around the 1968 Democratic National Convention, Hoffman confirmed that he'd talked about spiking the city's water supply with the hallucinogen LSD, but only

38 Ken Silverstein, "Homegrown Horror," *The American Prospect* (January 3, 2015).
39 Jessica Eve Stern, "The Covenant, the Sword, and the Arm of the Lord (1985)," in *Toxic Terror*, ed. Jonathan Tucker (Cambridge, MA: MIT Press, 2000).

as an empty threat. On the stand, he had the following exchange with his lawyer Leonard Irving Weinglass:

> WEINGLASS: Directing your attention to approximately two o'clock in the morning, which would now be Monday morning, do you recall what you were doing?
>
> HOFFMAN: I made a telephone call to David Stahl, Deputy Mayor of Chicago at his home. I had his home number.
>
> I said, "Hi, Dave. How's it going? Your police got to be the dumbest and the most brutal in the country," I said . . .
>
> I said, "I read in the paper the day before that they had 2,000 troops surrounding the reservoirs in order to protect against the Yippie plot to dump LSD in the drinking water. There isn't a kid in the country," I said, "never mind a Yippie, who thinks that such a thing could be done."
>
> I told him to check with all the scientists at the University of Chicago—he owned them all.
>
> He said that he knew it couldn't be done, but they weren't taking any chances anyway. . . .[40]

A valid point. Why take any chance with public safety when danger's in the air? And so, in the middle of the night on May 13, 2013, when a Massachusetts State Police trooper on routine patrol came upon two cars parked near an entrance to Quabbin Reservoir, the source of most of the drinking water for the city of Boston, he reasonably wondered just what might be going on. He then observed seven people walking out of a no-trespassing section of the reservoir property. He stopped them, and in short order he and his superiors learned that the midnight visitors were citizens of Pakistan, Saudi Arabia, and Singapore.

40 Douglas O. Linder, "Famous Trials," University of Missouri-Kansas City School of Law, accessed 2017: http://www.famous-trials.com/chicago8/1326-hoffman

This occurred at a time of heightened worries about terrorism by foreigners. A couple of months earlier two men with Chechen names had set off lethal bombs near the finish line of the Boston Marathon, and just days earlier the FBI in New York had arrested a Tunisian man for threatening to kill as many as 100,000 Americans by releasing toxic bacteria in the air or water.

Nothing came of the Quabbin incident. The seven midnight visitors were recent chemical engineering graduates of nearby University of Massachusetts and Smith College who were apparently on an ill-advised field trip. Meanwhile, health officials concluded that anyone aiming to poison a 410-billion-gallon reservoir would have needed truckloads of toxins to cause any harm.

Supporting that theory, no American reservoir has ever been successfully poisoned. Neither has any dam been taken down by a terrorist blast. But among the people who look out for water and public safety, precaution has become part of the day.

On a late summer afternoon a couple of years ago, I was interviewing an artist while standing on the grass-covered earth dam that holds back the waters of Roaring Brook in Babbidge Reservoir. The setting is remote, the only mark of human activity being a dirt road leading up to the dam, the dam itself, and a small, locked brick building on top of the dam that's decorated with graffiti. The forty-acre reservoir behind the dam is banked entirely by trees. The setting is untouched by fences, towers, walls, warning signs, electric wires, and light posts. It's a pristine and remote New Hampshire lake.

As the artist and I were talking about the various techniques of painting a water scene, a pickup truck came up the dirt access road and pulled to a stop. It was the same road that pranksters had used seventy-five years earlier to set off young Bill Hooper's alarms about enemy wrongdoing.

The orange vehicle carried the markings of the city of Keene public works department. Two men got out, and while one of them appeared to be looking over the dam from the side of the truck, the other walked over to where the artist and I were standing fifteen feet from the water's edge and asked in a conversational tone that conveyed a sense of authority overlaid with a veneer of awkwardness, "I have to ask you this, but what you are doing here?"

OUT OF THE TANK

After its waters leave Roaring Brook they enter another stream and then a river that heads south to the small town of Winchester, New Hampshire, at which point the river passes by the setting of a landmark case of industrial pollution.

In 1977, the Environmental Protection Agency contracted with a leather-processor in Winchester to try out certain waste discharge equipment. The idea was to help come up with national standards for the management of chemical-laden tannery waste, and the A. C. Lawrence Leather Company represented a seemingly excellent choice for a test. The company, which was a recognized supplier of hats and gloves for American pilots during World War II, was a major employer in town, and its daily discharge of 300,000 gallons of effluent would provide a prominent laboratory for pollution control technology.

For a couple of years, in return for hundreds of thousands of dollars of federal grants, tannery personnel filed reports about their emission control tests when in fact the managers there occasionally bypassed the treatment equipment entirely and instead discharged chemical-laden waste directly into the Ashuelot River.

The discovery of this practice led to the nation's first major federal criminal case that involved pollution. In 1983, five executives of the company were convicted of contaminating the river and falsifying reports about it; they were fined hundreds of thousands of dollars and given prison terms. Three of them also admitted to burying 1,000 leaking barrels of a suspected cancer-causing solvent not far from the river.

The director of the Justice Department's newly-created environmental crimes unit who prosecuted the case described the company's motivation: "It was profits—profits over people, profits over a public resource, profits over the public trust."[41]

The tannery shut down not long afterwards, and in the following years the EPA removed hundreds of tons of contaminated soil and chemicals from the site. Winchester's town government struggled unsuccessfully to interest developers in the property, which today is a forlorn setting of cracked pavement, chain-link fence, and unruly vegetation by the side of the river, a shocking memento of willful environmental abuse.

---

41 Ben A. Franklin, "U.S. Fines Tannery Polluters," *The New York Times*, April 30, 1983.

Industrial pollution still happens, rarely so brazenly but still often enough to remind us how exposed water is to chemical contamination. Not all rivers and streams are at risk, but a great many are, certainly those that flow by places where chemicals are used and stored. It doesn't help that we know extremely little about thousands of those chemicals, remarkably little about the condition of the tanks where those chemicals are kept, and breathtakingly little about the effects of those chemicals on the health of people. From time to time the dimensions of that ignorance come into full view, most recently in 2014 when two above-ground storage tanks on the banks of the Elk River upstream of Charleston, West Virginia, leaked 10,000 gallons of solvent into the river.

The contaminant in that case was a coal-washing solvent called methylcyclohexanemethanol, MCHM for short, and the site of the leak was a mile and a half north of the intake of the drinking water system for Charleston, the state capital. The incident was a nightmare of lax regulation, slipshod safety management, weasly business practices, and seemingly willful ignorance about the health effects of chemicals on the loose. The contamination set off alarms across the nation where countless oils, cleaners, gasses, and other unregulated chemicals are stored in tanks near rivers and streams.

The source of the leaks were two tanks that held 46,000 gallons of chemicals each. The tanks dated to 1938, and their bottoms had corroded. Apparently, the leaking had been going on for some time but had been slight enough to be absorbed by the underlying ground to no noticeable effect. But in January 2014, freezing conditions hardened the ground. Solvent pooled up on the surface and then worked its way beneath and through a defective cinderblock containment wall to ooze down the sides of eroded river banks; some of the solvent also got into the river through a deteriorated stormwater drainage pipe that ran beneath the tank farm property.

The solvent soon turned up at the Charleston water treatment plant downstream. The plant wasn't equipped to screen out the contaminant, which then made its way to sinks and faucets throughout the city, carrying with it a strong smell of licorice.

When people started talking, local government officials said they had no idea whether there was any reason to worry about the health effects.

The head of the privately owned utility that ran the treatment plant helpfully informed his customers: "We don't know that the water is not safe, but I can't say that it isn't safe."[42]

Within days and weeks, the sequence of disaster began playing out. Complaints of skin rashes, vomiting, migraines, and eye problems soared; residents were told to not wash their clothes in the water; schools were closed; downstream cities shut off their water intake pipes; local businesses closed; the White House issued a disaster declaration; the National Guard trucked in bottled water; the tank farm company filed for bankruptcy protection. Government health officials issued a "Do Not Use" order, then declared the water safe to drink, then reversed themselves and said pregnant woman and children were at risk. Waste from the spill cleanup was mixed with sawdust and dumped in a nearby city's landfill, after which neighbors there complained of smells, and the disposal companies were fined $600,000 and ordered to monitor for leaks for the next five years. In the months that followed, the West Virginia state legislature passed new inspection requirements for above-ground storage tanks, but shortly afterward critics gutted the new law. Injury lawsuits piled up, and six company managers including the president were convicted on pollution charges and sentenced to prison or probation.

The incident was startling not only for the distress that it caused businesses and 300,000 people in nine counties of West Virginia, plus the costs of cleaning up the mess and economic losses that ran well into the millions of dollars. The incident was remarkable for what it said about the limits of government oversight. Some of the tanks hadn't been inspected for twenty years.

The tank farm had previously been visited by state regulators after neighbors complained about a licorice smell in the air; the inspectors sniffed the air, took note of the smell and issued air-quality permits, but didn't inspect the tanks themselves.

Shortly after the incident, Rahul Gupta, the principal public health officer for the Charleston area, darkly said of the leak, "It can happen anywhere." Until then, most government regulations about chemical storage tanks were only about gasoline and other petroleum products that are commonly kept underground; in only about thirty states were

42 Ken Ward, "300K Lack Water in Southern W. Va.," *The Charlestown Gazette*, January 10, 2014.

above-ground storage tanks regulated at all, and in most cases that was only for fire code reasons and rarely out of concern for public health. Across the land there are tens of thousands of chemicals that, like the coal-washing solvent that got into West Virginia waters, weren't included in the EPA's inventory of toxic substances.

Suddenly, regulators across the country found themselves looking at thousands upon thousands of above-ground tanks, countless numbers among them old enough to be held together by rivets as the West Virginia tanks had been and containing chemicals that they knew little or nothing about. "We've been lucky that we haven't had more leaks," said Marshall Mott-Smith, a former longtime regulator of storage tanks in Florida who testified in vain three times in Congress to toughen up government regulations for chemical storage.

In Maine, one of many states that were jarred to action by the Elk River incident, regulators hired an engineering firm to map where above-ground storage tanks in the state were located. They expanded their drinking water protection areas from one mile upstream of drinking water systems to five miles. They called for training courses about what to tell the public when toxic leaks happen. Said Mott-Smith: "Elk River was a significant event that will affect how storage tanks will be regulated."

We should all hope so, and in that hope we can find confidence in what came of a tragic incident involving a storage container a century ago in Boston. In January 1919, a huge above-ground tank in the North End holding more than two million gallons of molasses collapsed. A twenty-five-foot-high wave of the stuff, which at the time was used mainly not as a culinary ingredient but rather as a component of explosives, rushed through the streets, killing twenty-one people. Investigations afterwards showed that the owners of the tank had known about structural weaknesses in the tanks but had done nothing about them.

The accident led to new laws. Boston city officials began requiring builders to include engineering and architectural calculations with their construction plans. These and other steps helped lead to stiffer building codes and storage tank regulations across the country.[43]

The rules that came out of the molasses tank collapse of 1919, then,

---

43 An excellent account of the incident and its aftermath can be found in *Dark Tide—The Great Boston Molasses Flood of 1919* by Stephen Puleo (Boston: Beacon Press, 2003).

foreshadowed the reforms and new protections that are coming out of the coal solvent leak in 2014. But there are differences. For one, the tank collapse in Boston was a single blunt-force cataclysmic event whereas the Elk River incident was a poisoning by one of thousands of chemicals that we knew little about—a disturbing fact in a country made modern by chemistry advances. For another, no one really knows where all those chemicals are being stored and could be leaking into the soil and air and water today.

Yes, there've since been reforms that placed more chemicals on government registries and do-not-spill lists, and there have been steps to account for all the tanks that hold them, including the moving tanks that are being pulled along by trucks and trains. But don't expect a full guarantee of safety. Said Mott-Smith, the former regulator who speaks from experience: "Humans are humans, and mistakes happen."

TEETH

When I was a young teen growing up in New York I went on a field trip to a natural history museum, and while most of my classmates were drawn to the big bones of mastodons or whatever, I remember being transfixed by a magnified drop of water. The display, which was a huge lit-up circle on the wall, had a zillion squiggles and dots in it. I don't recall whether the water sample came out of a stream or out of a tap, but I distinctly recall avoiding drinking any water for a couple of days after.

Research for this book many decades later confirmed that there are all sorts of things in water, some harmless and some not, including bacteria plus an occasional parasite, plus acids from the decay of leaves, then salts and traces of an array of minerals, one of them being fluoride.

In Roaring Brook, the naturally formed concentration of fluoride, which is an ion of the element fluorine, is extremely small, just at the level of detection of 0.1 parts per million, and for some people that's plenty.

Gerhard Bedding, who lives in Keene, New Hampshire, is one of those people. Bedding, a former teacher who's in his late eighties, first got to thinking about fluoride in the 1950s, not long after local governments across the nation began putting increased concentrations of it into their water for the stated purpose of improving oral health. He found the practice disturbing, initially because here was government doing something to drinking water without giving individual consumers a choice in the matter. He also found it unsettling that fluoride—a miracle cavity fighter by some accounts—was being delivered without regard to dosage. Says Bedding, "Doctors prescribe medicines by dose, but with fluoridated water no dose could be controlled." In that light, a person's consumption of fluoride is determined only by as much water that he or she drinks.

In time Bedding, who had long had an interest in science (his master's thesis at Wesleyan University in Connecticut was about Ralph Waldo Emerson and science) began becoming active in campaigns to keep fluoride out of public water.

In the fall of 2000, he was asked at the last minute to take part in a debate about water fluoridation in the town of Brattleboro, Vermont, a former industrial town about twenty miles to the west of where I live. Bedding, who was then in his seventies, had campaigned a year earlier against adding hydrofluorisilic acid—that is, fluoride—to the drinking water of Manchester, the largest city in New Hampshire, so he had some experience in the combat of ideas. Still, his resume was not equal to that of the expert whose debate chair he would be filling due to an unexpected change of schedule, nor was he as credentialed as the speaker he'd be facing. So it was with some trepidation that Bedding walked in front of the Brattleboro community-TV cameras to argue against fluoridation days before a local vote on the subject. His worries ended as soon as his adversary took the first question from the moderator, which was, as Bedding recalls it, "In fluoridation, what exactly is put in the water?"

The man responded with a long recitation of opinions about the benefits of fluoride to oral health and how cities and towns across the country had had good experience with it, and how a community without fluoridation was like a community without electricity or public sewers or driver's licenses, and so forth and so on, and at the end of the man's declamation the moderator turned to Bedding and asked if he had a comment, and Bedding responded: "I hope that you noticed what just happened. He had five minutes to answer the question but he never did." Bedding then went on to describe what goes into the water with fluoride, a substance that derives from the most corrosive and toxic element on the Periodic Table.

Not long after the debate, the residents of Brattleboro went to the polls and voted against fluoridating their drinking water, reaffirming decisions that they'd made twice before in the 1960s and 1970s—this, despite the fact that their energetic governor at the time, the doctor and future presidential candidate Howard Dean, had strongly encouraged them to make the change.

The subject of the vote in Brattleboro nearly twenty years ago was remarkable and still is. Aside from chlorine and related disinfection products, fluoride is the only chemical that humans put into public drinking water with good intentions, although some would describe those intentions as misinformed or cockeyed or, in the extreme, corrupt. Critics cast fluoride as nowhere near a nutrient or a remedy, but instead a poison that in excessive amounts can harm teeth, turn bones brittle and lead to attention deficit disorder, among other ills; on the other hand, proponents of fluoridation, including every US Surgeon General since the 1950s, say that fluoride is a proven protector of tooth enamel against bacteriological attack.

To put it mildly, people are of different minds about fluoridation. The division has played out over the years with all the subtlety of a religious war. The struggle can bring out the worst in the participants, meaning that if you were to step into this debate today you would find that there are only two places to stand: that corner over there with the stupids and this corner over here for the stooges.

It has been so ever since fluoride was introduced into the drinking water of Grand Rapids, Michigan, in 1945, and the controversy continues to span the nation. The very same day that Brattleboro voted against fluoridation in 2000, voters in thirteen other cities and towns across the country similarly said no to fluoridation while voters in nine other cities and towns said yes.

Consumers of fluoridated water include the 160,000 customers of the Manchester water works, which despite Bedding's campaigning to the contrary was authorized by slim majority in 1999 to add fluoride. In this region, the consuming population of fluoride doesn't include the 12,000 residents of Brattleboro, Vermont, nor the 24,000 residents of Keene who get only the naturally formed trace amount of fluoride in the waters of Roaring Brook. The situation in Keene has been formally questioned only once, in 1958, when the members of the Cheshire County Dental Society asked the city to fluoridate the water. The city's Board of Health responded, "In our opinion, the controversy as to the safety of fluoridation is not yet resolved definitively one way or the other. The Board of Health does not feel that it has the right to suggest supplying the general population with medication without its consent. It is possible for individuals to procure on prescription sufficient fluoride for their personal use."

The idea of using fluoridated water to battle tooth decay didn't come out of the blue, but there was disagreement over its origin. Some thought it came out of good science and enlightened health policy, while others felt it came out of flawed science and corporate greed.

The true origin lay in the early twentieth century when dental researchers went looking into why there were so many stained teeth in various communities in Colorado, Idaho, and Arkansas, among other places. The researchers eventually linked what was termed "Colorado Brown Stain" to very high levels of naturally present fluoride in drinking water. Further research turned up an unexpected secondary finding— that the people with brown-stained teeth had very few cavities. Hence the notion that low levels of fluoride can help protect teeth while leaving them white, and what better way to deliver that protection than through public water?

The addition of fluoride is incomprehensible to those who believe that, yes, fluoride may protect against cavities, but only topically, right there on the surface of the tooth. To ingest the stuff for the sake of good teeth is likened by some critics to eating sunscreen to avoid sunburn.[44]

So, is fluoridation smart? Studies show that it helps, particularly for families where tooth-brushing habits are generally poor and where dentist visits are rare.[45]

But in the debates about fluoridation, not all the arguments are about water and teeth, per se. There's a broader context. Gerhard Bedding grew up in Holland under Nazi domination, and he has an encompassing suspicion

44 Alyson Krueger, "Edible Sunscreens Are All the Rage, but No Proof They Work," The New York Times, August 29, 2016.
45 Recent New Hampshire state data show that the percentage of third graders who have tooth decay in the Keene area, where there's no fluoridation, is slightly higher than it is in the Manchester area, where fluoridation occurs. See New Hampshire 2013–14 Healthy Smiles—Healthy Growth Third Grade Survey: An Oral Health and Body Mass Index Assessment of New Hampshire Third Grade Students.

of government authority that includes other instances where things were added to what we consume—for example, many years earlier, direct and indirect pressure to add Vitamin D to milk (to fight rickets, a bone disorder), niacin to go into wheat (to block pellagra, a skin rash and also a contributor to dementia), and iodine to be added to salt (to prevent goiters).

Those ailments are now long gone from medical charts in the United States. Bedding acknowledges that rickets and other diseases have declined, but he bristles at the Big Brother approach. "When it comes to adding Vitamin D to milk or juice and 'enriching' other products, the big question right away is: What exactly is being added?" he said. "It's clear that vitamins can be produced cheaply as isolated chemicals, which are quite different from the complex composition of vitamins as they occur in whole foods. Education on choosing a good diet, to me, is preferable over government decisions to remedy problems by mandating additives."

As for oral health, Bedding grants that cavities have declined in recent decades, but he points out that Europeans, too, have also seen a drop-off in cavities and the vast majority of them don't drink artificially fluoridated water. The improvement, he believes, has come from better brushing habits, the formulation of fluoride in toothpaste and mouthwashes, and also better diets.

In Bedding's eyes, pouring fluoride into drinking water is an entirely different and more dangerous thing, and the government itself effectively admits that fact by advising parents of newborns against mixing fluoridated water with formula. Why run the risk of doing any harm at all, he asks. "Are we going to have science in our day and age?"

In demeanor—tall and elegant, a ballroom dance aficionado, well-spoken, twinkle in the eye—Bedding's an unlikely radical. In no way does he fit the mold of the nutcase in the Stanley Kubrick film "Dr. Strangelove" who ordered a nuclear attack on Russia after he became convinced that fluoridation, a suspected commie plot, had turned him impotent.

Bedding sees a different plot. In his view the government has abetted the industrial users of fluoride, chiefly manufacturers of aluminum and also fertilizers, in disposing of their toxic byproducts; in this view, fluoridation is the means of disposal and consumers are the chumps. "The fertilizer industry would have the darndest problem getting rid of waste [were it not for fluoridation]," he says.

Chapter 7
The Power of It
The remarkable evolution of hydropower,
and what it's meant to us

≈ ≈ ≈ ≈

THERE'S MORE THAN ONE WAY TO TURN A WHEEL

As the eighteenth century came to a close, Josiah Woodward, a Massachusetts man in his thirties, went looking for new beginnings in the interior of northern New England. He moved to New Hampshire and set up a farm, and in short order he built a mill a couple of miles northeast from where I live, where he used the power of water to cut wood and grind grain for an expanding population of pioneers.

The topography and geography had been waiting. Here were streams and rivers with big drops in elevation; here were soils and geology that kept water from leaching into the ground; here was plenty of rain to keep ponds and streams full, forty inches per year.

The region was made for waterpower, without which some towns might never have been built. Thumb through local histories in this part of the country and you'll find more than a few offers of money and land to millers who would move in and set a wheel turning. The absence of a mill in those days, wrote one commentator, was "inconsistent with the existence of community life."[46]

So it was that in 1820, when Woodward's mill was in its early years, more than 2,500 waterwheels were turning in New Hampshire, the equivalent of one mill for every ninety-eight inhabitants, the largest concentration of waterpower in the nation.[47]

And what variety! An early classic—"The Young Mill-Wright and Miller's Guide," a 400-page tome published in Philadelphia in 1795 and widely circulated during the next half-century—described the shapes

---

46 Louis C. Hunter, *History of Industrial Power in the United States, 1780–1930* (Charlottesville, VA: University Press of Virginia for the Eleutherian Mills-Hagley Foundation, 1979), 1:30.
47 Ibid., 37.

and forms of undershot wheels, tub wheels, breast wheels, overshot wheels, reaction wheels, cog wheels, and the myriad parts that went into them, all to put flowing or falling water to work. The patent office was flooded with ideas about how to make wheels that were better, bigger, stronger, cheaper, and more efficient, leading one late nineteenth-century skeptic to complain: "Every free-born American citizen considers it among his unalienable rights and privileges to invent a patent medicine and a waterwheel. And he usually does both with equal ignorance of and indifference to the laws of both hygiene and hydraulics."[48]

But who could be excused for giving it a try, if not by inventing a wheel then by making parts for one or putting one to work by the side of a stream? For thousands of frontiersmen, waterpower was a way out and a way up.

Downstream from Woodward's mill on Roaring Brook, two other wheels were put to work, and after the waters emptied into other streams and rivers on their way to the sea they powered a multitude of industries in the nineteenth and early twentieth centuries. At one time or another, within a day's walk from where Josiah Woodward had settled you could find makers of textiles, a pail maker, paper mills, producers of musical instruments, manufacturers of lawn mowers, makers of farm tools, a manufacturer of steam-powered cars, and more—each of them powered by the same flow of water that had set his wheel turning.

In the cycles of history all these enterprises ultimately went out of favor. There were practical reasons. The next time you come upon a sketch or a painting of a little mill by the side of a stream, a whisper of rustic simplicity, give a thought to what the artist might have left out. Likely: wood rot that required constant repairs, ice that froze machinery in place, fires, awful injuries, washouts, the occasional drought, and ultimately competition from larger mills in larger places that thrived on economies of scale.

Eventually even the big mills shut down as the economy evolved and new sources of power came on: coal, gas, nuclear. Where hydro once provided close to 100 percent of the nation's industrial energy, the proportion today is well below 10 percent.

That share might be heading back up. In 2016 the Department of

48 Samuel Webber, "Ancient and Modern Waterwheels," *Engineering Magazine* 1 (1891).

Energy predicted that electricity production from hydropower—already the single largest source of renewable energy in the nation—could rise by more than 50 percent by mid-century. Among the reasons: worries about the effects of greenhouse gasses and the promise of new hydro technology.[49]

That forecast came out before the current administration in Washington came in—an administration whose energy priorities embrace fossil fuels. But administrations last only so long. And the urge to invent is hard to suppress; just as there was a rush to new hydro methods and tools in the eighteenth and nineteenth centuries, recent years have brought an astonishing range of new ideas and new technologies to draw energy from water.

This chapter is about that recent rush. It's not a complete study by any means. Nothing here about turbines that are turned by ocean waves nor those that are activated by the tides. Nothing here about harnessing the kinetic energy of rain or techniques of pumping water into the ground to produce power-generating steam. This chapter is about only a few new methods, all coincidentally on the same flow of water—the very same flow that once powered the mill that Josiah Woodward built at the head of Roaring Brook two centuries ago.

Downstream from that starting point the stream's waters today enter a jumble of pipes and valves that doesn't look like hydro at all, yet that's what those pipes and valves are. Further downstream those same waters come upon dams that would seem to be too small to generate a single watt, yet they produce a lot more than that. Still further downstream, those waters are sucked a mile into the core of a mountain for a power-generating experience that can boggle the mind.

Our tour will introduce more than mechanical technologies that Josiah Woodward could never have imagined; it'll also show marketplace technologies and environmental practices that no one in his day could have fathomed.

≈

The starting point is Woodward's modest structure at the head of Roaring Brook. Picture it: a simple thing, the walls wood, the floor wood, the

---

49 "A New Vision for United States Hydropower," US Department of Energy Office of Energy Efficiency & Renewable Energy.

wheel wood. Hear it: the flup-flup-flup of the wheel turning, then the slosh of water spilling out, the flapping and slapping of belts, the whir of pulleys, the uneven rasp of an up-and-down saw doing its work on a piece of timber, and the grinding sound of a millstone turning.

That was then. What follows is now: three modern hydro installations that today use water that comes out of Roaring Brook, each put in place within the last fifty years and each with its own story.

POWER IN A PIPE

A mile and a half downstream from where Woodward's mill did its work, the waters of Roaring Brook today enter a reservoir. From there much of the supply gets sucked into a pipe that drops into a valley and then up over a hill where it enters the drinking water treatment plant run by the city of Keene, New Hampshire.

The plant is a no-frills brick structure next to an enormous green tank on a hill. The floor inside is washed-down concrete beneath a high ceiling. The water moves through pipes that are held together by nuts and bolts the size of golf balls, and the sound in the room is a roaring hiss that suggests the engine room of an ocean liner under full steam. Power's being generated here, but not in any way that you can actually see. The power's being produced inside the pipes.

The setup, the first of its kind and size in the nation when it was installed in 2011, arrived through a series of unexpected and unrelated events. It arrived as much of history arrives—out of accident, coincidence, curiosity, and timing.

The idea was born weeks after the terrorist attacks in New York on September 11, 2001, when two men were positioning a table near the window of an office building in midtown Manhattan. Looking down from forty floors up, one of the men, Frank Zammataro, took in the sight of water towers on the roofs of nearby buildings. He and his colleague casually wondered whether, in the event that electricity in those buildings ever went out, the water in those boxy tanks could be released to generate emergency electrical power to, say, keep lights on or keep elevators running.

Zammataro, a New Yorker who at the time was in his early forties, knew nothing about energy generation or waterpower mechanics. During twenty years on Wall Street he had picked up know-how in information technology before heading up marketing for a new wireless company. But the circumstances of the moment—a cousin had died in the terrorist attacks and Zammataro's business address two blocks from the World Trade Center towers had been rendered temporarily unusable—led to his wondering, *What if?*

He researched the water tank idea, and he eventually arranged a meeting at Rensselaer Polytechnic Institute up the Hudson River from New York City. He sketched out his thoughts on a napkin for a small group of academics and asked, "Is this something that can be done?" The immediate answer was no: A building-top storage tank would hold too little water to generate enough back-up power to do anything. But afterwards one of the professors took Zammataro aside and suggested that he look not to water dumping out of a rooftop tank but instead to arrangements where water is moving constantly under intense pressure from one place to another, and where the water pressure has to be reduced lest it do damage where it's headed. The professor suggested that he focus his attention on the spot where the conversion in pressure takes place, a heavy steel contraption that's called a pressure reducing valve, and see if that could be put to use generating electricity.

In 2003, on the strength of that advice and after field trips to water utilities in Virginia and Pennsylvania, Zammataro incorporated an enterprise that he called Rentricity (the name being a combination of the words "renewable" and "electricity") and he built a business plan that was based on the principle that somewhere in innumerable public water systems the pressure of water coming in from a reservoir under the force of gravity has to be reduced, and the pressure at that precise point of change can be captured to turn a turbine.

Zammataro opened his new business in 2005 and was awarded a patent in 2006. Five years later, he helped revolutionize the water treatment plant in Keene, New Hampshire, to generate most of the electricity that it needed for its own operations from the water coming in from reservoirs in the neighboring town of Roxbury.

The city of Keene had been ready. The community of 24,000 people already had a green reputation, having captured methane gas releases from its covered-up landfill to power the recycling center there. The small rural city had also set idling limits on government vehicles, a policy that means something to workers in a region where subzero days are part of every winter. In 2007, City Hall set a goal of meeting one-half of the community's energy needs from local renewable resources in twenty years. Pushing that dream, the city authorized a study to see whether water flowing into its water treatment plant could be used to produce electricity. The research concluded that, yes, a generating system could supply all of the treatment plant's electricity but at a capital cost of $550,000.

The price put the project well out of reach—it would take taxpayers more than twenty years to pay off the investment—so the idea was put on the shelf. But then, confirming that timing can count for something, months later a national economic crisis that originated in the housing finance sector led a new president in Washington, DC, to launch an $800 billion stimulus program to pull the economy out of the ditch. The American Recovery and Reinvestment Act was put in motion, and Washington went looking for what it called shovel-ready public projects. The power generation idea for Keene's water treatment plant fit the bill. It came off the shelf, and, thanks to the boost of $275,000 in federal stimulus money and Frank Zammataro's configuration, two companion turbines went on line in the 12,500 square foot water treatment plant in April of 2011.

Every minute of the day roughly 2,000 gallons of water from Roaring Brook flow into the system. The result: 50 kilowatts of electricity. The precise point of alchemy occurs where water surging in at 150 pounds per square inch is converted to a flow of ninety pounds per square inch.

The year after installing the system in Keene, Zammataro entered a competition in Dublin, Ireland, put on by an organization called the Global Cleantech Cluster Association. The contest attracted engineers from around the world with new ideas about waste processing, solar power, waterpower, and biofuel technology. Rentricity's design won the Best of Water Prize. A wordsmith at the event lauded his design as "a new stage of clean [by] applying higher resourcefulness to resources."[50]

For all its modern technology, the project in Keene's water treatment plant was like the Woodward mill that preceded it in a couple of ways.

Each was in on the beginning of something new. Josiah Woodward's mill went up when waterpower was transferring labor from muscles to

---

50 Cindy Yewon Chun, "New Green Technologies Hope for Fast Track Development," *The Architect's Newspaper* (January 4, 2012).

gearing that turned millstones and lathes and saws, a revolutionary thing. And Frank Zammataro's project wrings energy from flows of water that had previously been too piddling to fit into any equation.

Also, Woodward's nineteenth-century operation was small, generating at most three horsepower—enough to power tools that were only a few feet away. Frank Zammataro's twenty-first-century hydro installation is small, too, and it also produces power for immediate use.

Zammataro's hydro-in-a-pipe design went on to win plaudits at still more energy competitions as he went about installing turbines in half a dozen water treatment plants in North America.

But the business didn't grow as fast as the prizes and accolades had seemed to promise. There were reasons, one being that few new ideas, technological or otherwise, are immediate hits. Then too, the people he was pitching to—the operators of public water departments—already had plenty to occupy their days what with storing and cleaning and delivering water twenty-four hours a day. Add the cost, which wasn't cheap: most of Rentricity's water treatment projects, including the first one in Keene, needed a subsidy to get built.

Zammataro is convinced that his design will pick up momentum, but only after more government officials insist on energy savings in their spending. He said, "I hope that one day this will be a best practice, that no (water project) will be complete without an energy recovery consideration."

Meanwhile, he expanded his marketing to other fields, starting with irrigation projects in the West. Next in sight: poultry processors and manufacturers that use lots of water in their daily operations. The prospects are vast enough to keep him and several competitors going.

And why not? Every day in the United States 200 billion gallons of water run through pipes connected to water treatment systems, farms, and factories. Zammataro puts the business potential in the United States alone at $10 billion. "It's a huge market," he said.

A LIGHT TOUCH

After the diverted waters of Roaring Brook leave the water treatment plant in Keene, New Hampshire, they're shunted into mazes of underground pipes to sinks and toilets and restaurants and factory operations in the city. Eventually the waters come back together at a wastewater facility, and from there it's into the Ashuelot River south of the city. The flow meanders through farmland, passing beneath iconic New England covered bridges, before it takes a sharp turn to the west where it enters the field of vision of Bob King, hydro man.

King, who's in his fifties, came to waterpower early in life. He was eleven. On a Thanksgiving Day walk in 1972, he and his family came upon the remains of a power station on the Assabet River about twenty miles west of Boston near where they lived. The building was a wreck, broken windows and all, but the boy was immediately taken by the idea of the thing: power from nature.

The Thanksgiving Day discovery was the first of three events during the 1970s that sent King toward a life in hydropower, the others being an oil embargo that showed Americans how much they depended on imported petroleum for energy and then the passage of the Public Utility Regulatory Policies Act, a law backed by President Jimmy Carter that, among other things, pushed for renewable energy, hydro included.

In time King went on to study mechanical engineering at Cornell. He spent a college summer on a mill restoration project near home, and after graduation he worked for a spell for a company that made hydroelectric equipment. In the mid-1980s he moved to the site of a disabled hydroelectric plant on the French River in Connecticut—the small operation had been knocked out of commission by an awful storm in the 1930s—and he spent three years putting it back together and then running it before selling to a Massachusetts couple.

King went on to own and operate a handful of other waterpower operations in the Northeast, each small and without the towering dams and massive transmission systems that are what most people picture of hydro. His installations were mainly in a category that's called run-of-river, which generally means either no dam or only a small one. The operations generate electricity when rivers or streams are running strong, but in the driest days of summer they might not produce any electricity all. By design, then, run-of-river hydro is generally seen as having a light environmental touch.

This light touch appealed to King, who grew up in an environmentally minded household and who continues to hold a romantic view of rivers.

In casual conversation he gushes about the "spirit of a wild river from the mountains to the sea." Less poetically, he says, "Moving water really floats my boat." The light touch, too, is consistent with his thinking about energy generally in which he favors solutions that are small and individual—for example, better insulation in the attic of your home. Run-of-river hydro, then, was a natural.

Since 2007, King and his partner Tim Taylor have owned two run-of-river hydro operations about a mile apart on the Ashuelot River as it flows west to meet the Connecticut. The smallish dams hold back not much water, in one case a pond of just eight acres and in the other almost nothing. The dams date from the nineteenth century when they supplied local paper companies with mechanical power. They were abandoned when the manufacturers turned to purchased electricity in the twentieth century. In the 1980s, with interest in renewable energy rising, a Colorado-based hydro company took over the dams and outfitted them with turbines. A flood disabled the operations in 2005, after which King and Taylor bought the properties, fixed them up, and got them going again.

The small powerhouses are squarish wood-sided structures with nobody in them. King controls them electronically from his home twenty miles away. The operations represent something new in waterpower, less for their physical character than the modern marketplace technology that assures them customers.

The buyers of King's generated electricity include three Massachusetts towns and a university many miles away. Those customers, guided either by philosophical preferences for green energy or legal requirements, buy at least some of their electricity from sources that are green—and not just any shade of green.

King's operations meet certain terms that are laid down by an organization called the Low Impact Hydropower Institute in Lexington, Massachusetts. Since 2000 the organization has certified which hydros meet particular environmental standards. For King that means such things as assuring that there are enough trees on the riverbanks to keep erosion in check and whether the water above and below his dams contains the right levels of phosphorous and oxygen and also whether kayaking humans and fish can easily make it up and down the river.

Meeting these requirements isn't cost-free; fish ladders don't come cheap. Meanwhile King's got different people saying conflicting things into his ears. Environmentalists tell him they want leafy canopies of trees on the banks of rivers so as to keep waters cool for coldwater fish such as trout. Meanwhile, government regulators tell him they don't want to see trees anywhere near dikes and dams lest their roots damage the structures and cause safety problems.

King, a can-do and upbeat man, doesn't seem overly burdened by the pressures. He soldiers on at his hydro installations and for several years he looked into setting up a tiny hydro at a former milldam in his hometown of Keene as a demonstration project for the public. His timing's been good. Early in 2013 the House of Representatives in Washington took up legislation that, among other things, would stimulate small-scale hydro by lightening up the regulatory load. The Hydropower Regulatory Efficiency Act passed; the remarkable thing is how it passed. The vote, in a Congress that seemingly couldn't agree on anything, was 422–0. Ron Wyden, a senator from Oregon, summed it up: "You almost feel like [the] vote took place in an alternative galaxy."

PUMPED UP

Our tour so far has stopped by waterpowers that are small. Josiah Woodward's mill high on Roaring Brook was the size of a two-car garage. The turbines in Keene's water treatment plant could fit into the back of a pickup. Bob King's power stations on the Ashuelot River are each the size of a backyard storage shed, and his dams barely disturb the flow of water.

The next and final hydro installation on this tour, five or so miles further downstream and now in the south-flowing Connecticut River, is different. It's enormous, although that's not the immediate impression. At the river's edge there's neither a massive dam nor a hulking transmission station to be seen but instead a park-like setting with picnic tables and trees and a notice on a bulletin board about how eagles have been returning to the area. The tip-off is a set of security cameras on poles near a small parking lot at the edge of a cove. That's pretty much all you can make of a setup that arguably could have been sketched by Rube Goldberg, the twentieth-century creator of imaginary mechanical contraptions.

For six or eight hours of most nights, water is pumped out of the river through pipes that lead a half mile into the core of Northfield Mountain near the town of Turners Falls in northwestern Massachusetts. The insides of the mountain have been dug out into an immense cavern ten stories tall. It's a colorful setting of blue floors and four huge pumps painted a cheerful lime green. Workers move from here to there in diffuse light, the pumps behind them vibrating noticeably when the water's moving through, and in the control room other workers have their eyes trained on banks of screens and dials. The place could be a villain's command post in a James Bond movie, and in fact a movie is about as close as you can get these days since access by the public has been pretty much restricted for security reasons since 9/11.

If it's nighttime, the pumps in the cavern are sending the water straight up an 800-foot vertical pipe to a reservoir on the top of the mountain, elevation 1,200 feet. There the water sits, billions of gallons in a 300-acre lake, waiting for its hydro moment. The moment arrives sometime in the morning. At the flick of a switch, millions of gallons plummet back down the vertical pipe and into the same pumps that sent them up in the first place, only now the machines are functioning as turbines, at which point the water is sent rushing back out to the river.

The technology is called pumped storage, and its place in the big picture of energy production is to generate electricity only when it's needed. Most big producers of electricity such as nuclear plants or coal-fired plants have to run steadily twenty-four hours a day, but most of their customers such as factories and offices and homeowners use electricity mainly during the day, choosing to sleep at night, most lights out, machines off. Pumped storage plants, of which there are forty in the country, send water up to reservoirs when the country is sleeping, and release the water back down to generate electricity when the country's awake or when emergency outages occur.

The math that supports this technology is a bit unusual, some say nutty. The pumped storage plant uses more electricity sending water up to its mountaintop lake than it produces when the water's falling and turning turbines. The logic is in the timing. Northfield uses other producers' electricity to power its pumps when demand and wholesale prices are low—that's generally at night—and it sells its generated power into the regional grid when demand and prices are high, generally during the day. By storing water in its mountaintop reservoir, then, Northfield stockpiles energy for when it's needed, in its case 1.2 million kilowatts of electricity, enough to meet the power needs of nearly a million customers. It's a battery that's widely considered to be more efficient than any other energy storage technology—compressed air, flywheels, electrochemical capacitors, and so on.

The Northfield plant went into service in 1972 as what was then the largest such operation in the world. The same year about twenty miles north on the opposite shore of the Connecticut River, the Vermont Yankee Nuclear Power Plant was turned on. No coincidence there. Back then a fair number of nuclear power plants were starting up or being planned in New England, and because those plants operate at a constant rate day in and day out it made sense to find a place to store their output at times when demand for energy in the region was low. That's where pumped storage came in, first at Northfield and then at a slightly smaller pumped storage plant on a different river not far away.

Nuclear power in this country today doesn't have the future that it had back then; plants are being closed, not built. In New England, where the 620-megawatt Vermont Yankee nuclear plant was shuttered in 2014 and where other nuclear plants are on track to go offline, Northfield's owners saw their major source of power disappear. Nimbly, they fashioned a switch. In place of storing energy from producers that had to run constantly twenty-four hours per day, they proposed running their pumps increasingly on power from generators that ran only intermittently, meaning solar and wind. They also proposed expanding their water storage atop Northfield Mountain.

So far, this passage about the Northfield pumped storage plant hasn't included the word "environment." If I were to introduce that word, I'd first mention 1,000 acres of conservation land that the pumped storage people promised to buy and put in state hands back when they were pitching the project in the 1960s; that land was in addition to all the acreage that they would need for the power project itself. I'd also bring up the vast recreation arrangements on Northfield Mountain that the developers pledged for cross-country skiers and hikers and snowmobilers. I'd also bring up the nature classes about insects and birds and water and trees that the power producer today offers local children.

These nature-loving features were pitched at a precarious time for the pumped storage industry in its early days. Only recently had a utility in New York run into a buzz saw of citizen opposition to a plan to carve up a mountain on the side of the Hudson River for a pumped storage project. With that noise in the background, the team of New England utilities behind the Northfield project took pains to show a friendly face. Their powerhouse wouldn't deface the side of a mountain as the Hudson River project would; it would be built *inside* a mountain. Plus, there was all that new conservation land that would come with the project. And then there was this truly original and magnificent element: The developers proposed a mountain-top lake that was bigger than they needed for their own power requirements. The lake would be connected to a nine-mile-long aqueduct that would transfer water to the Quabbin Reservoir, the major water supply for the eastern part of the state. What a plan! Three hundred and seventy-five million gallons per day effectively sucked out of the Connecticut River when it was running strong, then pumped up to a mountaintop reservoir and then sent by gravity to Quabbin and water consumers in and around Boston sixty-five miles away. What timing, too! An extended drought had dropped Quabbin's water levels to perilously low levels. Technology and the Connecticut River would set things right!

This bold extra, which was called the Northfield diversion, never happened. The end came down to a political thing about bailing out urban folk in and around Boston with a resource that presumably belonged to the rural part of the state. Better instead to repair water pipes in the city that were leaking millions of gallons per day.[51]

The effective demise of the Northfield diversion in the 1980s ended one tension associated with the pumped storage project, but other concerns eventually surfaced. Local environmentalists apparently were okay with the project when it was first proposed twenty years earlier—back before the days of environmental impact statements—but they didn't stay that way as concerns about what it was doing to the river mounted. People began talking about erosion of the banks of the river whose water levels rose and fell by as much as four feet depending on the plant's operating

51 Good background can be found in "The Northfield Mountain Pumped Storage Project Counterpoint to Con-Ed" by Charles H. W. Foster, *Harvard Forest Paper No. 19* (Cambridge, MA: Harvard University, 1970). The paper details the differences between a failed pitch to build a pumped storage project at Storm King on the Hudson River in New York and the successful Northfield project.

cycle. There were questions about fish getting sucked into the pipes leading to the pumps. There were questions about the upstream and downstream impacts on the river itself.

Not a lot of people paid attention to these sorts of questions early on, and that's understandable. The Connecticut River, after all, had been dammed for centuries. What more harm could possibly come from using its waters to turn yet one more set of wheels—waters that to a large extent were already being backed up behind a conventional power dam downstream of the Northfield project's intake pipes?

When you read the early reports about hydropower that comes from pumped storage, you don't find much worry about the effects on where the water comes from (rivers mainly). The earliest environmental concerns mainly had to do with all the land that had to be sacrificed to make a pumped storage project—hundreds of acres for reservoirs and land for powerhouses.

But as river science and environmental sensibilities matured, people began looking closer at the effects on the river. How could they not, what with the Northfield plant regularly flushing water in and out at the rate of 15,000 cubic feet per second?

Those concerns got even sharper as the plant recently came up for a renewal of its federal operating license. In the course of the review, the Connecticut River Conservancy, the major environmental watchdog for the 400-mile-long river, suggested that the plant leave the river alone and instead build a separate and dedicated pool of water from which to draw its daily supply.

Now there was an idea. There are about fifty new pumped storage projects being considered in the United States today, and the designers for more than half of them intend to get their water not from rivers but from free-standing pools in an arrangement by which water circulates back and forth between a lake at the bottom and a lake at the top, no river involved.

The idea wasn't entirely new, actually. In 1981 a major federal report said that such dedicated pools made sense, particularly pools that were built below ground.[52] Underground storage probably isn't a possibility in

---

[52] Dames and Moore, "An Assessment of Hydroelectric Pumped Storage," for the US Army Corps of Engineers Institute for Water Resources (1981), 1–2.

Northfield, given the lay and structure of the land, but in other parts of the country such arrangements can make sense—in some cases in a distinctly satisfying way. More than a few of the new projects under consideration would store their water underground in old coal mining pits. That makes for an intriguing sequence. Waterpower—the nation's initial industrial power in the eighteenth and nineteenth centuries—was eventually supplanted by steam, and here the source of the fuel for that steam—coal —would help set hydropower rising again.

TRANSFORMATIONS

Early mills did more than produce product. They also changed lives. A Connecticut woman who fled the family farm for a cotton mill in the nineteenth century, recalled: "I had no hope of riches, but felt that there was something better within my reach and I must have it or die in the attempt. I began to realize that my future would be largely what I made of it, that my destiny was, as it were, in my own hands."[53]

Another woman who gave up hand-stitching shoes at home to take a job in a textile mill, said, "You cannot think how funny it seems to have some money."[54]

Here was social transformation of the most personal sort—money in the pocket, circulating with the opposite sex, chances at self-improvement and so on. Then too, the hours were long, the air bad, the monotony stifling, and the injuries awful. Wrote one observer of life in the mills, "It lies half in sunlight and half in shade."[55]

But mill workers, many of them girls and women, found an independence that wasn't available at home. And when the shade got to be too much—after factory owners began pushing for longer hours and cuts in pay—women left the mills and entered the expanding world of teaching, leaving their benches in the textile mills to waves of immigrants from Europe whose descendants ultimately helped transform the ethnic character of New England.

53 William Moran, *The Belles of New England: The Women of the Textile Mills and the Families Whose Wealth They Wove* (New York: Thomas Dunne Books, St. Martin's Press, 2002), 5.
54 Mary H. Blewett, *Men, Women, and Work: Class, Gender, and Protest in the New England Shoe Industry, 1780–1910* (Champaign, IL: University of Illinois Press, 1990), 44.
55 Benita Eisler, *The Lowell Offering: Writings by New England Mill Women (1840–1845)* (New York: W. W. Norton, 1998), 77.

The transformation was economic, too, as the center of gravity in New England shifted, in the elegant terms of historian Samuel Eliot Morison, "from wharf to waterfall."[56]

This chapter is about some of the changes that waterpower brought about as it powered the nation's early years by scaling up. The story of Nutfield, a settlement near the Merrimack River in New Hampshire, is a striking case. Rustic and rural, named after chestnuts that were growing in abundance, Nutfield took on a succession of names as honorees came and went and boundaries were adjusted. In time, Nutfield's proximity to waterfalls in the river caught the attention of industrial planners and investors in Boston. Fields and forests were acquired and packaged, streets were laid out, buildings were built, at which point the place received its final name—Manchester—the American iteration of England's great manufacturing center. The ultimate transformation was spectacular: Where chestnut trees had once grown, Amoskeag Manufacturing Company's Mill No. 11 had 17,000 workers on the job on more than 400,000 square feet of factory floor, the largest cotton mill in the world.

From these experiences you could draw two starkly different pictures of waterpower in New England: on the one hand, tiny operations in the outback such as Josiah Woodward's, and on the other hand, complexes of colossal buildings where armies of regimented workers turned out textiles by the mile.

There was yet a third picture, a quintessentially American picture: the middle place, neither city nor village, out of the way but still influential beyond its borders thanks largely to the power of water.

There's Salisbury, Connecticut, today mainly a residential retreat for wealthy New Yorkers. In the 1770s the community was, as boosters put it, the "Arsenal of the Revolution." The town owed its founding to the discovery of iron ore down below, but it owed its reputation to the operation of blast furnaces up top that supplied 80 percent of the cannons used in the Revolutionary cause, their bellows powered by creeks and streams that ran through town.

Other small communities won their time in the sun thanks in part

---

56 Samuel Eliot Morison, *Maritime History of Massachusetts—1783–1860* (New York: Houghton Mifflin, 1921), 214.

to flowing water. Rumney, New Hampshire, population 1,500, today mainly a rock climber's destination, was celebrated a century ago as the "Crutch Capital of the World." Five mills along a single stream turned out thousands of pinewood crutches on a weekly basis for customers on both sides of the Atlantic until aluminum competition came along; the last Rumney crutch maker went out in 2002.

Another town: North Easton, Massachusetts, nickname Shoveltown. At one point in the late nineteenth century, mills there produced 60 percent of all the shovels that could be had in the nation, its factories powered by a brook that for parts of the year was no wider than a path winding through the woods.

It wasn't waterpower alone that put these communities on the map. Economic success has many ingredients: the availability of raw materials, access to capital, a supply of labor, the timing of external influences such as wars, the resiliency of markets, the health of trade partnerships, and the arrival of brilliant pioneers and people who gather around them. There's also the underlying culture to account for, which in New England meant a respect for work and education that sustained the belief that one could—no, should—strive to improve one's lot. Here was New England's Puritan heritage talking: invent, and if not invent something entirely new then improve on someone else's invention. In 1902, a bulletin in the Twelfth Census reported that from the start of the modern patent system in 1836 through 1900, New England routinely generated more inventions per capita than any other part of the nation. "Industrial demand and invention go hand in hand," the bulletin observed. "They act and react, being interdependent."[57]

In the six states of New England that meant a lot of industry going on, much of it powered by water. Eventually the waterwheels stopped turning, not for lack of industry or water but for the arrival of a new technology: steam. Unlike hydro, steam needed fuel, yes, but it freed factory owners from having to build near streams and the disruptions that came with them: droughts, floods, ice.

But in the chronology of things waterpower came first, and for that reason little towns that had streams running through could make something of themselves. Had steam power come earlier in the industrial

---

57 Twelfth Census of the United States. Census Bulletin. No. 242., Washington, DC, 18.

era, one writer put it, "many towns and cities . . . would never have been much more than summer resorts."[58]

There's a small town on the eastern flank of Vermont on the way up to Canada that was transformed by waterpower in a remarkable way. Windsor, population today 3,500, was settled in the 1700s around a number of streams where mills turned out wood products, ground grain, and processed wool—standard production. In time, waterpower helped secure for Windsor something grander than basic self-sufficiency; it helped win the town a prominent place in the transformation of the nation into an international industrial superstar.

When I first walked Windsor's downtown not too many years ago, the words "prominent place" did not pop to mind. A roadside plaque marks the tavern where the state of Vermont was carved out of New Hampshire and New York in 1777—sure, no small thing—but my first impression from a stroll past empty storefronts was that Windsor had had better days. But what better days they were! You can find glimpses on the other side of a bridge that spans Mill Brook. There's a brick building several stories tall. Go in. The building, which once housed the biggest mill in town, contains the collection of the American Precision Museum, a carefully arranged inventory of mechanical instruments, lathes, sewing machines, typewriters, pumps, rifles, gun-making machines, and industrial gauges. All those products were made in this town.

Geographically, Windsor is positioned near the northernmost point of what came to be known as Precision Valley, a stretch along both sides of the Connecticut River 130 miles south to Hartford, Connecticut. For quite some time that long sweep of territory was the economic and technological equivalent of what Silicon Valley is to the nation today.

The reputation was grounded in an historic shift of manufacturing from the hands of craftsmen to the hands of machinists. Instead of making products by the piece, entrepreneurs up and down the Connecticut River, as well as in some other parts of New England, began making products in pieces; here was the idea of making interchangeable parts for pumps, firearms, clocks, sewing machines. It was an efficient method, the first intimation of mass production and the assembly line, and the output was

---

58 Malcolm Keir, "Some Responses to Environment in Massachusetts," Bulletin of the Geographical Society of Philadelphia, July–August 1917, as quoted in Ralph Brown, *Historical Geography of the United States* (New York: Harcourt, Brace, 1948), 153.

guided by standards of uniform detail so exact that, say, when a soldier on a distant battlefield needed to replace a broken trigger he and his superiors could be confident that the replacement piece would fit just right.

Windsor supplied firearms and parts of firearms to American soldiers in Mexico, British soldiers in Crimea, and Yankees fighting Johnny Reb, but the town's claim to fame came not from merely making firearms but from making the machines that made the components of those guns. Manufacturers in Windsor made milling machines, metal cutting machines, drill presses, lathes, rifling machines, gauges, calibrating instruments, and other devices that enabled factory production to be kept at the tightest tolerances. The quality and reliability were such that in the middle of the nineteenth century you could find Windsor-made machines and Windsor-trained machinists—the Windsor name—in cities practically everywhere.

As to why little Windsor would arrive at such distinction, being way up in Vermont, distant from markets, labor, capital, and other essential elements of industrial success, much of the answer flowed down Mill Brook, a stream that dropped sixty feet over the course of one-third of a mile as it entered the village from the west.

Of course, Windsor's success ultimately owed to the people who moved there and worked there, not to water in a stream. But without the power that could be drawn from that stream few factories would have been built, few inventions tried, few entrepreneurs and innovators clustering in one place to build off each other's collaborative and competing energies. Success fed on itself as a population of skilled machinists expanded; when they weren't making guns and gun-making machines, they were turning out sewing machines and other machines and tools for civilian uses throughout the Northeast.

In 1922, Guy Hubbard, a grand-nephew of one of the earliest inventors in Windsor, sourced the town's success to geography, specifically to Mill Brook as it emptied into the Connecticut River. The outlet caught the attention of travelers on the river, precisely the sort of people who could make change happen. Hubbard called them "pioneers in whose veins flowed the blood of Mark Twain's 'Connecticut Yankee.'" [59]

---

59 Guy Hubbard, "Leadership of Early Windsor Industries in the Mechanic Arts" (paper, Vermont Historical Society, Windsor, VT, September 1922).

Times change. You won't find machine-tool makers in Windsor today. In the 1880s, its biggest manufacturer moved to a nearby town for tax breaks. Windsor's history didn't end there, however; history can have momentum. Other factories tapped the local supply of skilled labor that earlier manufacturers had created to meet the production requirements of two World Wars. Even companies outside machine tool-making thrived thanks to space having been left for them by earlier industries. In 1936, Goodyear Tire and Rubber Company moved into an empty factory in Windsor and put upwards of 1,000 people to work making heels for shoes for military and civilian markets for the next half century as the town's population swelled to close to 4,500. More recently, in 2003, a maker of high-tech water filtering devices moved into the empty section of a machine-tool factory that had had its day before it itself closed a dozen years later. Other businesses gravitated to Windsor. Simon Pearce, a high-end glassmaker with 150 employees that was initially drawn to the area for its waterpower, has its headquarters there. There's a distillery. There's a big brewery. There's a hospital. There's a railroad stop—an inheritance from Windsor's big days.

As for Mill Brook, it flows on undisturbed and also, as can happen, sometimes disturbed. In August 2011, Tropical Storm Irene turned the rivers and streams of Vermont into torrents that caused $600 million of damage. Mill Brook, gone wild, ripped apart a streamside park that volunteers for the American Precision Museum had completed just two weeks before, tossing around heavy granite steps as if they were little plastic dominoes. The scattered remains of the park are just yards from where, more than a century earlier, water had had far more productive purposes—making machines, making a difference in people's lives, making a name for a small town way up in Vermont and helping turn the wheels of growing nation.

NEW VALUES

For much of the twentieth century, Americans accepted, even celebrated, the idea of big solutions. A classic example: the massive Grand Coulee Dam in Washington state, 550 feet high, a mile wide, and holding back a lake of 125 square miles. In 1941 Woody Guthrie, on a paid propaganda commission from the government, sang a loving salute that included the lines: "Grand Coulee Dam, Boys, Grand Coulee Dam/I wish we had a lot more Grand Coulee Dams."

You won't hear lyrics like that today in the United States. No big dams are being built in this country, and some are being taken down as a result of new thinking about hydro's effects. Even the smallest hydro operations have come up against new values and new ways of thinking.

Several miles east of where I live you can find the small town of Harrisville, New Hampshire. It's a postcard-pretty mill town thanks to a remarkable preservation effort that was launched by the family that ran the mills there for more than a century. The result is a fully functioning community that, in addition to being designated a National Historic Landmark, includes a locally owned yarn supplier and maker of small looms, artists' studios, offices, and a grocery that puts on elegant dinners once a month.

The center of Harrisville is structured tightly around a brook that gets its start in a lake north of town and then winds through marshy flatlands before pooling up in a pond, after which it drops one hundred feet over the course less than a quarter mile, passing by and through a succession of mill buildings. In an efficiency move in 1947, the mill owners stopped using the water to help run the looms and turned entirely to electricity that came in over power lines. Decades later, however, the waters of the brook were set to go to work again.

Shortly after Harrisville's last woolen mill shut down in 1970, the village caught the eye of John Hansel, a New Jersey manufacturer of water chilling systems who was looking for a change. He moved his Filtrine Manufacturing Company to Harrisville and set about reviving waterpower in town.

Hansel found a second-hand turbine in a defunct mill operation in Cazenovia, a small, upstate community in New York, and he installed the 180-kilowatt machine in the old wheel pit of one of the mill buildings that he'd bought. The step was in line with his personal inclinations toward self-sufficiency. Soon after his move to New Hampshire, Hansel built a home at the top of a 750-acre property that had no electrical connections. He installed a wind turbine and propane and diesel generators in a strategy that involved stocking his garage with one hundred batteries to store the juice. His home, then, was entirely off the grid. But his efforts to generate his own power at the mill were substantially less rewarding.

For every hour that it was operating, Filtrine needed electricity, and for every hour that the company wasn't open, it needed none at all. In line with the traditions of water-powered mills, Filtrine would store water in the mill pond until it needed power. Hence, the water level in the pond would fluctuate when the turbine was put to use. Rising and falling water levels in mill ponds had always been a fact of life in such towns, but the people who had come to live around Harrisville Pond in more recent years weren't accustomed to such irregularity. There'd been no waterpower in the mills for decades, after all, and people who had bought and built cottages on the water had gotten to depend on the level being constant and not rising and falling like the tides.

So when Hansel cranked up his turbine to supply his factory with electricity, the water levels in the pond dropped, and this led to complaints from pond-side residents. Tensions over that, plus struggles with federal power regulators over whether Hansel had to get a license to generate energy even if the electricity was only for himself eventually led him to give up on the idea. In time a frustrated Hansel left town, taking his company with him, leaving the turbine behind. For a strong-willed man who was accustomed to having his own way, the failed stab at waterpower was a deep disappointment.

"I thought it was the greatest opportunity of my life, to restart the mill," he recalled years later.

On Hansel's departure, the mill buildings were purchased by a preservation group that included descendants of the long-time mill-owning family. Money was raised for restorations, and eventually the group turned its attention to the turbine that Hansel had installed.

Taking a cue from Hansel's troubled experience, the preservation group pledged to run the turbine not on the basis of how much power they needed on a particular day, but on what it would take to assure that the water level in the mill pond didn't fluctuate. It was an accommodation to modern sensibilities: if the pond wasn't being adequately refreshed by rains and snowmelt and flows of water from upstream storage, the turbine simply wouldn't be put to use.

Still more accommodations had to be made to get waterpower restored, and these were less easily arranged. The Federal Energy Regulatory Commission came calling, and its agents asked questions that no one would have given a thought to back when the mills were in their heyday, such as what about the impact on historic resources and what about the effect on any endangered species of animals that might be living there?

It took years for the project to grind through the regulatory process. The eventual cost of getting a license, which included the cost of consultants, engineers, drawings, studies and so on, came to $54,000.

How different this was from a century earlier when mill operators could generate all the power they needed when they needed it, with scarcely a thought to anybody else, except perhaps farmers downstream who had cattle to water.

The population of parties who have a say in waterpower today is big. Every written communication about the Harrisville project today must be copied to thirty-six agencies of government at the local, state, and federal level, including the Bureau of Indian Affairs, and the city of Keene, which isn't even in the same watershed.

John J. Colony III, a direct descendant of the founders of the mill whose quest to restart waterpower ultimately took eight years, told me at one point, "It was like we were building the Hoover Dam. But we weren't changing much. We were just hitching it up."

Colony, a man of the world, leans green. And he believes in limits. A couple of decades ago, for example, he helped block the construction of a state highway through his rural community. He concedes that early mill operators probably paid too little heed to their impact on their surroundings, but getting permission to restart a turbine in the mill took him through a regulatory process that was far more cumbersome, byzantine, and costly than he'd ever expected. A man given to understatement, he said, "I was a little surprised."

In the course of things, other surprises surfaced. The second-hand 1936 turbine in the mill turned out to be decrepit and inefficient; the restoration group, Historic Harrisville, wound up going for a new turbine for $450,000, most of which got covered by other companies through a state system of tax breaks. As for who would oversee the new machinery, a recent retiree to the town came looking for something to do. Serendipity: the man had the right skills. Said Colony, "When the history of Historic

Harrisville gets written, there'll be a big chapter about luck."

The new, bright blue 38-kilowatt Francis-style turbine started work in early December 2018 in the granite-walled wheelhouse of the mill.

The impact was immediate. Historic Harrisville's power bill for that first month came to $612.47, mostly for fixed charges, down from $2,311.28 the preceding November. Given the half-million-dollar outlay for the new turbine, the savings would still make for a ridiculously long payback. But savings weren't the point except to help keep rents down for artists and others who now use space in the mill. The main thing was the restoration of waterpower. The main thing was a return to energy self-sufficiency—an ambition that under certain circumstances can be more complicated than you might think.

Our values change. They evolve. And they can come into conflict. For example, water levels in the mill pond used to rise and fall depending on the factory demands of the day, but that's no longer okay to people who live around the pond.

As for diverting water from a stream to turn a wheel, nothing new there except for the laws and regulations and personal expectations that can come with environmental awareness.

Then this question, which is not so much about waterpower itself as it is about the energy independence that the waterpower represents. The installation of the bright, gleaming blue turbine in the old granite wheelhouse was about what—a return to energy self-sufficiency? By that interpretation, would it be okay to take other steps to keep energy production local such as, well, put solar collectors on the roofs of aesthetically authentic nineteenth-century buildings in town, or put windmills on the ridgelines of local hills where today only trees grow?

The question in this historic mill town gets to what the new turbine represented and what values it ought to be judged by. No one's yet asked if solar panels and windmills have a legitimate place in town, but at some point they reasonably will.

"It's an interesting question," says Colony. "This is an industrial town."

Chapter 8

Inventive Minds

Innovation in the water world

≈ ≈ ≈ ≈

HOW WATER CAN LIFT ITSELF UP A HILL

If you were to make your way alongside Roaring Brook, you'd eventually come upon a piece of granite in the bed of the stream. The stone, a cleanly cut rectangle about four feet long and seven- or eight-inches square at the ends, is out of place among rocks that have been rounded smooth by eons of water washing over them. But in fact, the piece of granite askew in the stream once had a very real purpose. It was part of a dam for a set of remarkable pumps that enabled water to pump itself up hill.

The granite and the pumps date back to shortly after 1835 when Samuel Wadsworth, a gentleman farmer in southwestern New Hampshire, was out riding an unruly colt on a winter's day when he was thrown and killed. He had just turned fifty-two. His homestead, including a stately brick-and-granite house up on a hill, wound up in the hands of Seth and George Wadsworth, the eldest of his eight children. During the next twenty years, the two brothers made a number of improvements to the property, including one that would qualify them in modern terms as being early adopters of technology. They found a spot in Roaring Brook that ran along the lower part of the estate where they used the piece of granite to form the dam, and just below the little dam they installed two devices that pumped water uphill to service the Wadsworth house and barns.

The pumps used no electricity, this being too early for that; neither did they use steam, diesel, wind, or human or animal muscle. Ingeniously, the pumps used only the force of water flowing into them and the resulting air pressure inside to send the water uphill. The devices were called hydraulic water rams, and their design was so startling that the *People's Cyclopedia of Universal Knowledge*, an ocean of information for the inquiring mind that was published in New York in 1879, placed water rams on a list of

BENSON'S PATENT WATER RAM.
No. 1.

The above is a representation of *Benson's Patent Water Ram*, for raising Spring or other water for supplying Towns or Farms.   By means of this Ram, persons having a small branch or spring, that will afford one gallon of water per minute, with a small fall, can have a portion of it, or any other water, raised to his house or barn, through a small leaden pipe.   This Ram will raise twice the water that any other forcing pump will, with the same water power —there being only three valves to keep in moti place of the heavy water-wheel and piston. Ram can be driven by branch water and raise s or branch water to the house at pleasure, by ti a stop, without any derangement of the Ram, very simple and easy to keep in order—the v being faced with leather and easy of access, c replaced by any farmer—there being no othe that can wear.

No. 2.

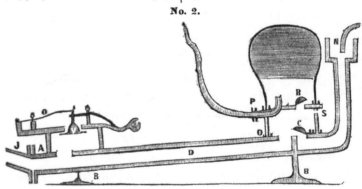

"Benson's Patent Water Ram" from *The American Farmer*, Volume 1, No. 10, 311, April, 1846

the most important technology innovations since the beginning of recorded history, along with the invention of glass by the Phoenicians, the formulation of gun powder, the design of the printing press, the invention of the clock, and fifty other groundbreaking ideas.[60]

The water ram got attention in the *Cyclopedia of Universal Knowledge* because its function was simply amazing. Water in a stream flows into a small chamber two or so feet tall; the force of the water rising in the chamber creates air pressure within the enclosure that causes a valve on the side to open for a fraction of a second, forcing a bit of water into another pipe that's headed slightly uphill; the continuing flow of water coming in helps rebuild the air pressure in the chamber, which pushes the valve open again and forces more water into the inclined pipe, and so click-click-click-click, small amounts of water are pumped up a hill—in the Wadsworths' case, one hundred feet vertically over a lateral distance of more than one hundred yards.

The ram is important to this book for its early place in a seemingly endless stream of inventions around water. The innovations continue through today with contraptions that pull power from the movement of tides, and machines that squeeze drinking water out of fog, and also breakthroughs in hydro technology that protect fish from the whirring blades of turbines, and sensing devices that remotely monitor the performance of water wells in jungle settings, and more. When you consider the full scope of invention in and around water, it's a patent office bonanza.

Among all these inventions, the ram stands out for having lasted the ages. They're being built and installed today in much the same form and shape as the first versions in the eighteenth century. I've been in touch with American Mennonites who are installing hydraulic water rams in Congo villages. Peace Corps volunteers have used them in Panama. I've spoken with a man in Texas who designed a subterranean ram to lift water up to the parched surface from a cavern beneath an aquifer in the ground. As recently as 2013, a man on a farm not far from where I live used a ram to pump water up to a greenhouse to irrigate his lettuce.

In another town, I came upon an out-of-service ram that's housed in a small wooden structure downhill from an elegant hilltop home. The estate

60 *People's Cyclopedia of Universal Knowledge*, III (1882 revision): 1987.

was built as a summer retreat in the 1880s by a St. Louis man who made his fortune in tobacco. One of his great-granddaughters took me to the spot, now surrounded by forest, and she distinctly recalled the kathunk-kathunk-kathunk cadence of the pumps as they sent water up the hill as late as the 1940s. She also remembers her mother saying that the sound turned the horses skittish.

One local man I know, the owner of a couple of small hydroelectric stations, keeps a water ram in his garage. Bob King, the hydro man who appeared in Chapter 7, happened upon the device years ago while helping clean out an old warehouse in Connecticut. On a recent sunny day, he hauled the sixty-pound pump out of the back of his garage and set it out on the driveway for some show-and-tell. He mentioned that his family owns country property a few miles to the east where goats used to graze. With a gleam in his eye of a packrat who knows he's got something special on his hands, he enthused, "I imagine one day that this'll lift water again!"

Most people today know nothing about water rams. The clerk at your local plumbing supply store would likely draw a blank if you asked about one. A shame. The invention has a long and distinguished history.

The instrument dates to 1772 in England, but credit for developing the self-acting water ram goes to Joseph Michel Montgolfier, a Frenchman, in 1796. He was a man of inventive bent, having teamed up with his younger brother Etienne a decade and a half earlier to pull off the first known manned ascent of a hot air balloon.

The water ram idea soon crossed the Atlantic, and in 1809 the first American patent was issued to two New Yorkers. But the device remained pretty much an incidental fancy until the 1840s when technical improvements—plus publicity, mainly through periodicals aimed at farmers—stirred public interest. Here was technology doing fantastic things: You could water your livestock without having to lead animals down to a stream; you could irrigate your crops by literally lifting water up a hill; and you could supply your kitchen with water without having to crank a pump.

The first recorded demonstration of a water ram in New England took place in 1846 in western Massachusetts. Not long afterwards, Seth and George Woodward purchased their models and installed them in Roaring Brook.

In time, hydraulic water rams were in use across the country irrigating fields, filling bathtubs in homes, even supplying the rush of water to fountains in fancy gardens.[61]

The idea of the self-acting water pump excited the American spirit of innovation, and a flurry of improvements appeared. In 1871, Christopher Hodgkins, who lived not far from where the Wadsworths were sending water up a hill, was awarded patent No. 119,764 for a water ram refinement. An experienced inventor already with a sewing machine patent in his pocket, Hodgkins continued to work on water rams, winning a second patent and opening a factory to manufacture the devices in a neighboring town.

Within several decades, however, the introduction of yet another new technology pushed hydraulic water rams to the side. Here was electricity, installed first in cities and then strung into the countryside through rural electrification campaigns. The wondrous water ram receded from general consciousness as property owners on hilltops turned to electric pumps and also, eventually, diesel-powered pumps that were easier to maintain and that could handle comparatively greater volumes of water. In 1956, three-quarters of a century after the water ram was listed as one of the most important innovations of all time, a published history of American technology made no mention whatsoever of the device, distracted as the author understandably might have been by such intervening miracles as the telephone, motion pictures, the airplane, the automobile, antibiotics, and atomic energy.[62]

Yet the low-tech water ram hung on. *Popular Mechanics* magazine published articles about the device in the mid-1930s, and the first oil embargo in the early 1970s reignited public interest. A story in *Mother Earth News* in 1973 that hailed "perpetual motion for the homestead" reported: "Although water won't run uphill, some exceedingly clever soul discovered a long time ago that H2O can be persuaded to pump itself in that general direction. The hydraulic ram pump makes it possible."

With *Popular Mechanics* and *Mother Earth News* as sources, the water ram has a garage feel, something for the do-it-yourselfer. That's understandable but also limiting, because in the hands of some people

---

61 Arthur Channing Downs Jr., "The Introduction of the American Water Ram, ca. 1843–1850" in *Bulletin of the Association for Preservation Technology. 7*, no. 4 (1975): 56–103.

62 John W. Oliver, *History of American Technology* (New York: The Ronald Press, 1956).

this invention from the past has a large and promising future.

Chief among those people is Auke Idzenga, a marine engineer who first laid eyes on a water ram while doing technical training in his native Holland in the early 1980s. The idea of water lifting itself without external power fascinated him.

In 1985, in a dramatic career change, Idzenga left his job at a shipping company in Holland to move to the island of Negros in the Philippines for community development work. He soon observed the troubles of hilltop farmers who lacked electrical power to pump water to their plots during dry seasons. At this point he remembered the water ram from his training days back home. Drawing on his engineering skills, he designed a lightweight version that could be easily assembled from locally available materials such as door hinges. His first installation was for a tenant farmer up a hill. Idzenga looked to a stream at the bottom of a slope where he built a small dam that delivered water to a ram pump; the ram sent water vertically more than one hundred feet to irrigate lemongrass plants and service a piggery and a fish-growing operation.

Idzenga secured Philippine patent protection for his design, and, in time, corporate and government underwriters helped him and a new organization, which he called the Alternative Indigenous Development Foundation, install rams in hundreds of upland villages in the Philippines. His work eventually gained international attention, and he was asked to install rams in Afghanistan, Nepal, and Colombia; meanwhile, his factory shipped models to a dozen other countries in Europe, South America, Africa, and parts of Asia.

In 2007, Idzenga was invited to a ceremony at the Royal Geographic Society in London put on by a British nonprofit organization called Ashden. Since 2001, Ashden had been running an annual competition for innovations in sustainable energy and development, and Idzenga had been nominated for his lightweight water ram and also his system of training local people to install and maintain the devices.

The awards, which that year were handed out by Al Gore, went to a variety of organizations for such things as tiny water-powered mills in Nepal and biogas plants fueled with food waste in southern India. As it turned out, Idzenga's ram didn't come in first in its category. That distinction went to a group in Bangladesh that designed solar-powered flat-bottom boats to ferry materials to poor rural communities and that also outfitted villagers with solar equipment and bicycle-powered water pumps.

Still, the second-place honor gave Idzenga's nonprofit organization added visibility, and in subsequent years it received similar recognitions from other international groups. He expanded the line of water rams to nine different models, and meanwhile added solar water-heating devices, low-cost biogas plants, foot pumps, and micro wind turbines to the mix.

The water ram stands at the top of that list, partly because it can be built from mainly local materials and partly because Idzenga was able to modify its size to meet a range of requirements. Some of his gravity-powered pumps are small enough to supply a single household, while others can deliver water to whole villages. In 2013, to help mark its one-hundredth year of operations in the Philippines, the Coca-Cola Company underwrote a ram pump installation program that included, among other elements, a ram system that lifted 7,000 gallons of water a day 500 feet up steep terrain from the Pandanon River in Negros Occidental to service nearly 300 homes and an elementary school.

That, says Idzenga, is just the beginning. An intense man with a clear sense of needs, possibilities, and practical realities, he said, "My dream is to have the ram pump technology spread and be known as a solution for upland water problems anywhere in the world."

The water rams that he's installing around the world are descendants of the very pumps that the Wadsworth boys used to lift water out of Roaring Brook, a century and a half ago. Only today those pumps are long gone; just the piece of cut granite remains.

I came upon the granite while hiking the length of Roaring Brook one summer's day. I took a guess on following the line that the pipes would have taken to the original Wadsworth homestead. All I had in hand was an ancient sketch of the town, an historical note about the rams, and a compass, no map or GPS, but after a hundred yards of stumbling through thick forest on a slight upward grade, I came to a large cellar hole that was given over to nature with trees growing out of the middle. The place had been unoccupied for 130 years. I imagined a mother and child sitting in the house back before electric lights or plumbing or any other modern convenience was part of daily life. I pictured the mother giving the child a wash. Or maybe she was boiling vegetables. Perhaps the two were simply taking a drink of water on a hot summer's day. There they were, mother and child, and there was I in my hiking boots, apart in time yet brought together over a pump that sent water up a hill.

THE SEPTIC SIDE

Depending on the weather and season, most of Roaring Brook winds up getting piped to a drinking water treatment plant and from there it's distributed to homes and businesses in the city of Keene, New Hampshire, where it's put to countless uses, none so common as the flushing of toilets.

There are close to 20,000 toilets in the system, along with a network of sewer lines and pumping stations that lead to a wastewater plant. That's the standard design for municipal sewage systems but the Keene system, which on average processes three million gallons of wastewater per day, stands out for having on its payroll a man who wears a bright red cape on his shoulders, silver boots on his feet, blue rubber gloves on his hands, and a shiny metal hard hat. And if that's not enough, he also sings in the manner of Bruce Springsteen.

The man in the cape is Eric Swope, an otherwise soft-spoken fellow in his mid-fifties whose cape isn't part of his regular workday uniform but instead is what he wears in a music video that he wrote and directed with local high schoolers. The video draws attention to a modern consumer marketing success that increasingly bedevils wastewater people in cities across the land and Europe too, namely the disposal of facial wipes and similar products down the toilet that wind up clogging not only indoor plumbing but also entire sections of sewage systems; in the video he comes to the rescue with plunger in hand.

Swope's video, which is titled "Don't Flush That," is modeled after Springsteen's energetic version of "Pink Cadillac," and confirms that under the right direction even sewers can be entertaining. Hence:

> "... I'm talking 'bout your used baby wipes, cloth and
> paper rags, paper towels and wipes, fats, oils and grease
> and even plastic bags
> They don't go down in the swirl
> They clog the city's pipes
> You'll have overflowing toilets on a Saturday night..."[63]

---

63 https://www.youtube.com/watch?v=ZtKok9Ilelw

The video, which you can find online, was inspired by the Singing Sewermen of Thames Water in London who, since 2009, have been trying to discourage people from using their toilets as trash cans for what are called nondispersibles (kitchen grease, rags, wipes, and such) that wind up clogging the sewers at repair costs totaling more than $10 million per year. The problem got international attention in 2017, when a congealed mass weighing 130 tons clogged a section of London's sewer system; the rock-solid "fatberg" had to be removed with high-powered water jets.

Stuck pipes have long been a problem for sewer people due to the flushing of diapers, paper towels, dental floss, tampons, Q-tips, condoms, and even mopheads, but the situation's apparently gotten much worse in recent years with the discovery by marketers and manufacturers that adults could be enticed to use towelettes and facial wipes to sanitize their hands, remove makeup, and generally freshen up. It's a billion-dollar market, and it's growing.

Swope's music video has received good play on the local community-access TV station, and he's heard from a few people who have changed their ways. "At least some people are taking it to heart," he says.

As sanitation minstrels, Swope in Keene and the Singing Sewermen in London signal an important evolution at public wastewater systems. Originally sewer officials focused their attention solely on getting human waste out of neighborhoods and into rivers that floated it away; later they took on the added responsibility of separating and cleaning the waste before letting it go. The next point in this history, where they are today, is where wastewater managers look upstream and downstream of their plants. Upstream they're looking to control or otherwise limit what's coming at them, be it fats and oils from commercial kitchens, chemical waste from factories, or wipes and other personal care residues from private bathrooms. The effort is reflected all the way down to job titles that didn't exist all that long ago. Swope, for example, is called Industrial Pretreatment Coordinator. He visits factories whose waste streams of metals and chemicals can make it through sewage plants and then into rivers intact; he visits commercial kitchens to limit their releases of grease; he reaches out to homeowners whose wastes can clog pipes and send sewage backing up and spilling onto lands and into rivers. Between 1998 and 2006, the Department of Environmental Services in New Hampshire, one of the nation's smallest states, recorded nearly 700 sewer spills. Two results, in New Hampshire and elsewhere, are new rules about what businesses are allowed to discharge into sewers, and new technologies that trap or otherwise screen out contaminants before they can get into public pipes.

The advance of technology doesn't stop there. It also extends to the downstream side with what to do with the sludge that remains after water's been squeezed out and filtered and cleansed and sent back into the flow of a river.

In Keene's case the sludge was initially piled up for composting. The plant's at the end of a long drive past the city's airport and therefore a good distance from neighborhoods. But the area is in a valley where air inversions aren't uncommon, which means that the composting led to public complaints about stink. Today, the plant ships up to 150 tons of sludge per week to a landfill on the other side of the state that takes the resulting methane gas and puts it to use generating power for nearby homes. In a particularly innovative step, in 2009 the landfill was tied into a twelve-mile-long pipe to the University of New Hampshire where a cogeneration plant produces electricity for the five million square-foot campus, the first such setup at any college in the nation.

From all this—from the beginning of wastewater to its ultimate disposal—the range of invention on the septic side is seemingly limitless. That's been so since at least the design of the first flush toilet a century and a half ago, which inspired patents for toilet paper, toilet paper fixtures, toilet seats, toilet brushes, indoor plumbing, sewers, pumps, screens, filters, membranes, the countless variations of sewage treatment technology and the software that runs it, and eventually inventions for using what's left over, whether to generate electricity or to fertilize fields or to make biodegradable polymers that can be used to make plastics. These final uses indicate larger purposes in the sewage sector that justify a redefinition: Sewage isn't waste, it's a renewable resource. That's rather new: the methane gas from the landfill where Keene's sludge is trucked today was originally burned by the landfill operator simply get rid of landfill smells. Only later did new thinking and new turbines put the methane to use generating power and, meanwhile, cut down on the release of greenhouse gasses that in the atmosphere are far more potent than carbon dioxide.

I hadn't imagined any of this when I booked my personal visit to the local wastewater treatment plant a while ago. At the time I thought, well, poop conveyed by water. Then I heard about the technology and the costs of it and the problems that come with clogs; I met the caped man, only he was dressed in civvies. It wasn't until we were outdoors on the edge of a pool of swill that I got the sense of sewage as something greater. In the pool there was a little island of green floating around with stalks and leaves reaching up a foot or two, almost like a reverse oasis; the little island had formed on its own out of the ambient bacteria and was floating around, growing in front of my very eyes, ultimately to be fished out and discarded. It wasn't poop that I was seeing but instead nutrients in spontaneous action, signaling even larger purposes for something that we long disposed of as waste.

A LAUNDRY IDEA

In early 2014, three PhD students from Taiwan at the Massachusetts Institute of Technology in Cambridge, Massachusetts, joined up for a competition run by the school's Department of Materials Science and Engineering.

The event was one of an expanding number of technology and entrepreneurship contests at MIT, the first of them going back twenty-five years and the biggest one handing out $200,000 to groundbreaking innovations in the clean energy field.

The materials science contest, which is underwritten by Dow Chemical Company and Saint-Gobain, the French construction materials giant, is unlike other MIT competitions in that it requires a prototype; other competitions are mainly structured around business plans pitched to judges posing as potential investors.

In the materials science contest, the team of two women and one man looked first to the idea of capturing methane gas that's produced by cows. The concept fit the competition's focus on sustainability. Their idea involved installing the equivalent of a catalytic converter in buildings where livestock are kept and bottling their gasses in liquid form.

That didn't last long. "We didn't want to buy a cow," joked Alina Rwei, a member of the team, whose graduate work was in polymer science.

The students shifted their attention to waste and efficiency in the use of water, a subject about which they had some familiarity back home where people and businesses in some regions have to cut back on water use during parts of the year.

Sasha Huang, whose field was materials science, didn't come from one of those periodically water-short regions, but her household is conservation-minded anyway. Bathwater is saved and put to secondary uses such as flushing toilets and watering plants. "Instead of a single use, we should be able to use water multiple times and in a more efficient way," she explained. "I would say that this does affect how I think about water."

As they examined the use of water in households, the three team members got to thinking about water as an agent—a vehicle, a carrier of soap—at which point they spotted an opening. Most of the soap and all of the water that runs into dishwashers and washing machines comes out as waste. The challenge: could any of that water and accompanying unused detergent be recycled for another run through the washing machine?

The challenge was to pull dirt and grease from water before sending the water back for another cycle. The subject apparently hadn't been examined before. "Laundry is not well understood," said team member Chris Lai, who was working in chemical engineering. "We were going into a field that was unseen by the scientific community."

Lai and his colleagues came up with a filtering system that, when attached to a washing machine, can recycle 95 percent of the initial supply of water and detergent. Their math was appealing. By their calculations, it would cost approximately $52,000 to outfit a laundry in a 500-room hotel with a filtering and recycling device; the savings in water and detergent would pay for the investment in less than seven months.

In September of 2014, the team submitted its idea, now named AquaFresco, to MIT's materials science contest. It won the $10,000 top prize. Half a year later, AquaFresco took third place and $3,000 in a water innovation competition at MIT, finishing behind a system that remotely checks up on the performance of water wells in jungle settings and an in-home desalination device for application in India.

AquaFresco still has work ahead, starting with finding a hotel to test out its idea. And the students face still more research and testing to try out other possibilities such as helping factories and car washes recycle the water they use.

Of the students' innovation, Mike Tarkanian, an MIT instructor who oversees the materials engineering competition, said, "The value is there, for sure."

It most surely is, given recent water shortages throughout the country. More than just practical, the design is financially appealing for its reduced use of water as rates rise partly to repair old pipes that have been leaking water long enough.

Here, then, is where AquaFresco makes its mark: Unlike innovations that increase the supply of usable water—inventions that harvest water from fog, that draw drinking water out of sewage, that remove salt from water, and so on—AquaFresco aims to cut the amount of water that consumers use and, by extension, the volume of water that cities spend money to provide.

By that definition, AquaFresco is in company with one of the most far-reaching water-saving ideas of the last half-century, an innovation that's enabled public and private utilities and their taxpayers and ratepayers to avoid countless millions of dollars of spending on new water supplies.

In the 1980s, officials in Keene asked an engineering firm to scout out additional supplies of water for the city's 24,000 residents and local businesses. They were worried that their principal source, the Roaring Brook reservoirs, wouldn't be able to keep up with water demand ahead. The engineers drafted a plan to pull water out of a separate stream that ran along the bottom of a small valley and pump it uphill to be mixed with the Roaring Brook supply. The costs would be hefty. In addition to the expense of building a water collection point, there'd be the costs of pumping the new supply uphill; plus, there be new disinfection costs since the source of the newfound supply, unlike Roaring Brook's waters, was downstream from a public swimming area.

The new supply was never built. The reason: water consumption in Keene began slowing and then it fell.

The change resulted from economic change as some local factories either went out of business or trimmed their operations, reflecting national trends away from manufacturing. The major users of water in Keene today aren't the machine toolmakers and precision bearings manufacturers as before, but instead the local hospital and a commercial laundry.

But more meaningfully, households in Keene began cutting back their consumption of water, not out of any new consciousness about conservation but rather something more mundane, namely the plumbing fixtures in their homes. Increasingly, when people in Keene flushed their toilets or took showers or turned on their kitchen faucets, they were using less water than they had previously because those fixtures were now more efficient, a case being toilets that today use 1.6 gallons per flush—as little as one-quarter the volume that earlier designs had needed.

The change came mainly out of a new law that on the face of it would have seemed to be an unlikely vehicle for rules about plumbing fixtures in homes and businesses. In his final months in office, President George H. W. Bush signed the Energy Policy Act of 1992, a sweeping set of measures to reduce the nation's dependency on foreign oil. The bill included some obvious things: incentives for fuel-efficient technologies, electric power deregulation, natural gas imports and so on. But the law also stipulated that plumbing fixtures such as showerheads, faucets, and toilets use reduced amounts of water, the logic being that it takes energy to supply water that those fixtures use—notably toilets, which account for about 30 percent of household water usage—so why not require fixtures that use comparatively less water?

The regulations didn't appeal to everybody. Early-model low-flow toilets occasionally required two or three flushes to get the job done, so what was the point? Toilet designs eventually improved, but some critics never got over it. In 2011, fully nineteen years after the mandates about plumbing fixtures went into effect, Republican senator Rand Paul of Kentucky lit into a Department of Energy official in a hearing in Washington: "Frankly, the toilets don't work in my house. And I blame you, and people like you who want to tell me what I can install in my house, what I can do."

In fact, critics of the law did have a choice in the matter, and they still do. They could use chamber pots or outhouses, which is what a lot of people did before water began being piped to homes, hotels, and other businesses in the late nineteenth century, a modern miracle of public health that led consumers to use more water, ultimately by bathing more frequently and sprinkling their lawns and washing their cars. Before indoor plumbing, per capita consumption of water in the United States averaged ten gallons a day; with public water, daily use soared to more than ten times that volume, forcing cities to build or expand reservoirs, drill more wells and invest in expensive water treatment systems.

The low-flow fixtures helped turn around the trends of consumption. So too did redesigns of washing machines that came on in the 1990s. So, too, would the AquaFresco initiative. They're all part of a wave of experimentation and innovation that, if it's not pulling parasites out of water, it's turning sewer plants into generators of electricity or redesigning sidewalks to capture falling rain, even using dehydrated pumpkin or banana peels to pull heavy metals out of water—an endlessly expanding universe of invention.

In New England alone, this universe includes an annual Symposium on Water Innovation at Northeastern University in Boston, a Water Resources Center at Worcester Polytechnic Institute, the Water Innovation Prize at MIT, the Stormwater Research Center at the University of New Hampshire, the Water Innovation Network at the University of Massachusetts, the Water Resources Center in Rhode Island, and the Connecticut Institute of Water Resources. The universe includes money: in 2015, the governor of Massachusetts pledged $800,000 for water innovations, the goal being a technology cluster that can harvest some of the $500 billion of global outlays that go into water each year.

Spend enough time in this universe—the water technology competitions, the water conferences, the government institutes, universities with water innovation centers, the policy papers that tell of scarcity, the investment newsletters about infrastructure spending, the venture capital firms with slogans such as "Hydrocommerce Never Sleeps"—and soon enough a sense of déjà vu surfaces. A picture of the young Dustin Hoffman comes into view; the newly minted college graduate is being directed to a new future:

> Mr. McGuire: I want to say one word to you. Just one word.
> Benjamin: Yes, sir.
> Mr. McGuire: Are you listening?
> Benjamin: Yes, I am.
> Mr. McGuire: Water.
> Benjamin: Exactly how do you mean?
> Mr. McGuire: There's a great future in water. Think about it. Will you think about it?[64]

---

64 Paraphrased from *The Graduate*, a 1967 film by Mike Nichols, based on the 1963 novel of the same name by Charles Webb; in the print and film versions, the future is plastics.

Chapter 9
How Four Artists Found Their Causes in Water
In the footsteps of Thomas Cole and the Hudson River School

≈ ≈ ≈ ≈

INSTALLATION ART FOR WATER

In the third decade of the nineteenth century the nation's first recognized art movement began taking form. The movement, reverential in its celebration of nature, came to be known as the Hudson River School. The name was actually a catty insult by a critic who believed that the subject matter—hills, valleys, fields, rivers—was, well, just too provincial.

But nature in its unspoiled condition proved to be a welcome subject, first in and around the Hudson Valley and the Catskill Mountains and then up the White Mountains of northern New Hampshire. The appeal of the paintings was that they were not only about the wonder of nature but also the threatened ruin of it.

It was a time of change, with trains taking tourists to new resorts in the countryside and with industry putting out its pollution. Thomas Cole, the first figure in the movement, lamented "the ravages of the axe [as] the most noble scenes are made desolate, and oftentimes with a wantonness and barbarism scarcely credible in a civilized nation."[65]

Relevant to this book, water was an essential part of the tableau. Cole wrote that any landscape without water was "defective." He explained: "Like the eye in the human countenance, it is a most expressive feature: in the unrippled lake, which mirrors all surrounding objects, we have the expression of tranquility and peace—in the rapid stream, the headlong cataract, that of turbulence and impetuosity."

Benjamin Champney, another distinguished landscape painter, described a favored brook in northern New Hampshire as his "first love [where] many, many days and hours have I passed, painting and singing an accompaniment to its silvery music . . ."[66]

---

65 Essay on American Scenery, 1835.
66 Benjamin Champney, *Sixty Years' Memories of Art and Artists* (Woburn, MA: Wallace and Andrews, 1900).

These artists were part of the nation's early environmental awakening. Inspired by nature, they put their talents to the cause, and in those efforts they demonstrated that art can make a difference.

What follows are accounts about four other American artists who, in recent years, put their talents to work in support of water and made a difference. The stories are about more than paintings on a wall; in only one case are they about paintings at all.

The first of these stories begins not on a hillside overlooking a river valley nor by the side of a mountain brook putting out silvery music, but in an elementary school gymnasium in eastern New Hampshire.

The artist is a woman named Christine Destrempes. As we find her, she and her assistant have just finished setting up a video monitor on a small table when a door at one end of the room bursts open and in rush eighty chattering third and fourth graders, whom two teachers guide into a seated semicircle on the floor in front of the video monitor.

Destrempes, an energetic woman in her early sixties, is at Mast Way School near Durham, New Hampshire, the home of the state university's main campus. She's standing to the side of the video monitor, the screen of which displays the name of the Lamprey River Advisory Council, a nonprofit friends-of-the-river organization that's sponsoring her visit.

She introduces herself and she says a couple of things about the Lamprey River, a mostly forested river that starts in a small lake in the mountains and flows about fifty miles to the ocean, along the way passing several miles from the school. She asks a couple of questions to engage the students such as "Does anybody know what a watershed is?" and she gets some pretty good answers. She talks about how the river is used, including the fact that 37,000 people get their drinking water from it, and then she points to a different image that's come up on the screen. The image is three girls of about the age of the children in her audience; the girls are dark-skinned and barefoot, and they're carrying plastic water containers along a dirt road.

Destrempes explains that each day the girls walk about four miles from their village to fill up the containers at a well and then carry them back home with what will be their households' total consumption of water that day. She explains that since the girls have to fetch water every day they can't go to school, which means they'll have real trouble getting jobs when they get older. She points to a six-gallon plastic water container at her feet that's similar to the ones that the little girls in the picture are carrying and she asks whether anyone would like to try a hand at lifting it. There's an excited scurry as the children jump to their feet, and one-by-one the students hoist—and in a few instances fail to hoist—the nearly fifty pounds of water that's in the container, and then they return to their positions on the floor.

Destrempes tells the students that she's a printmaker and a painter, and also that she runs a small organization called Art for Water that tries to bring attention to the importance of clean drinking water. She displays an image of a recent art project and explains what it is. It's a steel-framed, open-sided cube that measures ten feet square at the bottom and is eight feet high. From the top bars hang thousands of clear plastic bottle caps strung together on fishing line. The structure represents what Destrempes understands are the nearly 14,000 people around the world who die each day because they can't get to clean water.

She tells the children that they're going to help create a different kind of art installation in which each of them will write something about water on a piece of paper, and the pieces of paper will be mounted all together on a wall at the local public library, the idea being that the display will help raise awareness about the importance of clean water.

Destrempes explains that in past times the Lamprey River provided energy for quite a few mills, and now, she tells the students, "Your words will generate energy."

With that, the assembly ends and the students go back to their home rooms. Destrempes and her assistant put away their video equipment and water container, and then they walk down corridors to a common room where they move onto the more active phase of their visit where art and water will intersect in the hands of children.

At the center of the room there's a rectangular surface area that's made up of small tables pushed together. As the assistant sets up trays and boxes of colored pens, Destrempes carefully empties a supply of textured cardstock onto a stand in the corner. The paper has been roughly torn into pieces in the shape of arcs and waves; the colors are soft blues, browns, yellows, grays.

In a minute or so, about twenty of the students from the original group of eighty show up with a teacher and they take their places standing around the big table. Destrempes explains that their job is to think up something to say about water, then write it down on scratch paper, taking care to get the spelling right, and then use pens to put their statements on the torn shapes of heavy paper.

The children immediately go to work in studious and quiet fashion. Some come up to get a second or third piece of paper. After about fifteen minutes, Destrempes gathers the students in a circle where one-by-one they read what they have written: "If the water goes, life goes with it." "Sip your share. Share your sip." "We are what we're wasting." "Protect our mother." And so on.

With that, Destrempes and her assistant collect the pieces of paper and thank the students for their work. The children leave with their teacher and within five minutes another group of students arrives for their turn at the table, and after them the other students. At the end of all this Destrempes and her assistant pack up all the papers and take them to the Durham Public Library where they add the young students' statements to those of local high school students that were generated earlier in the week. The statements are arranged in undulating waves that flow across a wall.

The installation, which Destrempes calls "The Stream of Conscience," remains at the library for a month, and then the contributions head to Destrempes's studio on the other side of the state where they're stored along with similar expressions on torn paper from prior workshops with church groups, schools, private parties, civic clubs, and an adult day care program for non-English speakers in a Hispanic section of Lynn, Massachusetts.

The inventory of statements about water will expand, as Destrempes takes her presentation to schools in other parts of the country with the support of grants, her aim being to open people's eyes to the fact that there are limits to the supply of clean water.

That her message got across at Mast Way School in Durham was confirmed by a letter that she later received from the mother of one of the third graders there:

"I wanted to let you know that your presentation made quite an impact. [Robert] spoke enthusiastically about what he learned when he got home from school that day, and since then, he has been very interested in conserving water at home. The part of your presentation that made the strongest impression on [Robert] was when you shared the story of how girls have to walk miles to retrieve water and then carry it back to their homes.... He was shocked to know that the girls didn't go to school, and he thought this was unfair."

A year later I got back to the mother to see whether the lesson had stuck. She replied, "Just the other evening, I was brushing my teeth in the same sink as [Robert]. I usually turn off my water, but I didn't this time as I was distracted. All of a sudden, [Robert] reached across me and gave me a 'you know better' look as he turned off the water."

Destrempes is relatively new to water advocacy. She was in marketing for many years before developing a name in painting and printmaking, and then one day in 2002 she came upon an article by William Finnegan in the New Yorker about a large-scale water privatization initiative in Bolivia that blocked poor communities' access to clean drinking water. The article, titled "Leasing the Rain," reported that more than one billion people around the world have no access to clean water and are subject to the ravages of waterborne diseases. The article added that the global demand for water is rising faster than the supply.

Destrempes, whose studio is on the edge of a small lake, says that she had been staring at water for a long time but she had never given much thought to it. She resolved to get people thinking about the problem of shortage, a commitment that took her to personal counseling and training to help her overcome fears of public speaking, and then began talking to people about what they can do about the problem. She admits to not having the answers. "People want me to tell them what to do, but I'm not a solutions person," she said. She sees her job as getting people to think about water—whether access to it or the wastefulness of bottling it in plastic—and leave it to them to decide what's next.

A PROCESSION DRAWS ATTENTION TO A POND

In 2007, acting on reports about people swimming and fishing in the industrially polluted waters of Mashapaug Pond, a kidney-shaped body of fresh water surrounded by grids of streets, homes, and businesses in

South Providence, Rhode Island, the state Department of Environmental Management put up warning signs that said in part:

Mashapaug Pond Do's and Dont's

To keep you and your family safe until we learn more, please do not:

> Drink pond water
> Eat fish caught in Mashapaug Pond
> Swim, wade, play, or bathe in pond water
> Boat whenever thick scum, algae mats, or foul odors occur on the pond

Rhode Island Department of Health

In short order, Bob Vanderslice, who at the time worked for the state Department of Health, heard complaints about the signs. For one, they were English-only in a city of wide ethnic diversity. For another, the signs had the impersonal feel of government decrees, which tended to invite vandalism.

In a moment of inspiration, Vanderslice turned to Textron Inc., the conglomerate that in the 1960s had acquired the assets of the Gorham Manufacturing Company, a longtime silver products maker on the shores of Mashapaug Pond. During the century preceding the modern environmental movement, Gorham had contaminated its grounds and the 114-acre pond with lead, solvents, PCBs, and other toxic crud. Textron had pledged to clean up the Gorham site at what turned out to be immense expense, and in that spirit it agreed to Vanderslice's request for $5,000 to underwrite better warning signage around Mashapaug Pond.

With money in hand, Vanderslice contacted the Rhode Island Council on the Arts, which in turn approached Holly Ewald, a local painter. To brief herself, Ewald stopped by community centers and schools, and, along with teachers and students she came up with a series of posters in English, Spanish, and Cambodian that are easy on the eye, light on text, and heavy on illustration, including one with a colorful but woozy fish with x's in its eyes.

After the new warning signs went up, Ewald's curiosity led her further into the neighborhoods surrounding the pond. She'd attended quite a few public meetings during which she noticed that the only people in attendance were government officials and representatives from Textron.

Residents who lived near the pond and whose families were exposed to the contaminated waters were nowhere to be seen. She recalls telling herself, "We need to do something on the street."

Ewald, who was then in her early fifties, had been involved in a street performance once before, as an art teacher for children in a Caribbean-themed parade in New Jersey. In Providence, she talked with local performers and others, and she came up with a parade that she called the Mashapaug Pond Procession.

Every spring since 2008, a line of street bands, dancers, super-sized puppets, marchers, children in fish costumes, and others carrying hand-made works of art has wound its way around Mashapaug Pond neighborhoods. The performance, which now includes artwork that floats on the pond itself, aims to spread the word about pollution in the waters and also instruction about how to keep things from getting worse, such as picking up dog waste, not feeding wildfowl, and also cutting back on lawn fertilizer, the residues of which can be washed into the pond by stormwater and cause algae to bloom.

The parade customarily draws a couple of hundred people plus onlookers. The preparation lasts weeks and includes classes in local schools where children learn about plankton and the cultural history of the area around Mashapaug Pond, which translates as "great body of water" from the Nipmuck language. The students also learn about the pollution of land and water by industry and how, under well-intentioned impulses, neighborhoods in the area were obliterated in the cause of urban renewal in the 1960s, their community histories wiped clean.

To Ewald, who now oversees the annual procession through a nonprofit organization, the parade is about more than art and more than water; it's about communities that over the years have been buffeted and bulldozed by humans. Among other steps, she's painted murals around a nearby Little League field, one of which depicts the landscape before an industrial park went in, and she's also had a hand in planting plum, pear, and cherry trees where orchards used to thrive.

"I feel like people really need to look at their own places and build off that," she explained. "I have a genuine passion for education through place."

Now occupying an office at Brown University, Ewald studies communities in various ways. She organizes oral histories. She researches what's happened to native Americans and immigrant groups such as Cambodians. Around Mashapaug Pond, her interviews form a record of generally forgotten times when the pond was central to daily life and when children caught frogs and splashed into the waters from rope swings and went out on rafts and skated on ice. Recalled one of her interviewees, an oldster who grew up near the waters: "The pond was the day."

There aren't many illusions about how far the recovery of the pond can go. It's in an industrial city, after all. From a distance on a sunny day the water looks blue, but close up it's not something you'd want to drink. Stormwater washes in pet waste and anything else that's left on paved surroundings. There have been sewer leaks. The chemicals that local industry poured into the pond can't all be scoured out. Then, too, contamination of a different sort continues as a stream coming in from a different town on the other side of a highway regularly feeds the pond with phosphorous. "It's probably never going to be pristine," said David Talon, the head of the local neighborhood association. But he said that he imagines a day when Mashapaug waters will be safe for boating and catch-and-release fishing. "We've seen some progress," said Talon, who's bicycled alongside the procession a couple of times, and who says that little if any improvement would have occurred if locals hadn't showed that they cared.

It wasn't the warning signs alone that got them caring. Recalling the early days, Ewald said that one of her first steps was to talk to the founder of a local street puppet group about how to stage a public event to draw attention to the pond. She recalled that he asked her directly, "Holly, do you want to do a protest or a celebration?" She said she responded, "I want to do a celebration. I mean, this is a beautiful pond and we need to clean it up."

A PAINTER HELPS PROTECT A LAKE

Evelyn Dunphy, a watercolorist in Maine, came to painting late. She'd been a stay-at-home mom, then she worked for Pepsi Cola outside New York City before moving to Maine in the late 1980s where she did market-ing for a surgical instrument designer. As for art, she'd had success making intricate hand-appliqued wall hangings, but Dunphy had always wanted to paint, and in 1995 she attended a talk about landscape painting. The following week she signed up for an evening class in painting at the local high school. She was fifty-five.

For the next five years, while still holding down the marketing job, Dunphy painted in her laundry room at home at night. In 2000, she turned to painting full time. A couple of years later she traveled into Maine's vast interior and set up her easel on the shore of Katahdin Lake, a 717-acre body of water that's accessible only by foot and floatplane, just east of the majestic mile-high Mount Katahdin.

"I totally fell in love with the mountain," Dunphy recalled of Katahdin, a magnificent piece of heaven in the middle of nowhere that translates as "greatest mountain" from Abenaki-Penobscot.

"I went every fall to paint at Katahdin Lake. I realized that if I wanted to be a full-time professional artist I would need to focus my work on a particular subject in order to make a niche for my work in Maine. I knew it would be Katahdin because of the mystery and magic that I feel about it. It truly has a magnificent presence."

The magnificence is enhanced by the lake's reflective waters. The setting had been stirring artists at least since the middle of the nineteenth century when Frederic Church, the landscape painter from the Hudson River School, first visited. He painted there several times and later built a camp on the shores of a nearby lake that also faced the mountain. His camp still exists in its rustic off-the-grid condition, and occasionally is a venue for painting workshops that Dunphy puts on.

In 2006, a couple of years after committing herself to Katahdin, Dunphy received a call from someone in the state Department of Conservation who'd seen her work. The caller invited her to meet some people who were putting together a huge nature-protection land deal. The group, which principally consisted of state government officials and figures from the Trust for Public Land, a big nonprofit organization that helps preserve outdoor spaces, was in talks to buy 4,000 acres around Katahdin Lake from a logging company. The price was $14 million.

The deal represented the chance of a lifetime that had eluded the one man who had had the resources to make it happen on his own. That was Percival Baxter, the son of a wealthy family in Portland, Maine, who, in the early 1920s, served three years as the state's governor.

Baxter is known for a number of things during his service in government, among them the appointment of women to state jobs and his naming of Jews and Catholics to government positions in the face of an ascendant Ku Klux Klan. And, at age forty-four, he was the youngest person ever to occupy the governor's office.

Baxter's name in Maine is tied principally not to these distinctions but to something else that he did on his own after he left office. Having failed to get the state legislature to conserve Mount Katahdin, he personally acquired more than 200,000 acres of land, including the entirety of the mountain, with his own money and gave it all to the state to be maintained as a public park. On his death in 1969, he willed $7 million to permanently finance the operations of Baxter State Park to forever assure that budget-cutters in the state capital would never have a say in what happened there.

The park, an expanse of mountains, valleys, forests, and lakes, is pretty much in the middle of Maine, a five-hour car ride from Boston. Serious hikers know of Katahdin as the northern terminus of the 2,100-mile Appalachian Trail that begins in Georgia. Baxter himself knew Katahdin as "the mountain of the people of Maine."

Despite his efforts, Baxter's ambitions for the park that bears his name were incomplete. He put together a great many land deals between the 1930s and the 1960s, but he never found a willing seller for the 4,000 acres of forest land on the shores of Katahdin Lake. The property, which contained some trees that were more than a century old, was simply too appealing to lumbermen.

Not that every logger felt that the lake lands should be cut. Marsha H. Donahue, another Maine painter, recalled a surprise visit from one of them in an unpublished history of her gallery near Baxter State Park:

"One day in the fall a foreman from the Gardner logging operation parked his truck across the road and came in the gallery just to look around. He was a workman and did not seem to have knowledge of art. He seemed to have something on his mind. I chatted with him and waited him out. Finally he said he had been working on a skidder on the north end of Katahdin Lake and he realized it wouldn't be too long before their crew was about a quarter mile from the edge of the lake. He had shut down his machine and walked to the shoreline and stood there for about 45 minutes, just taking in the beauty. He said it would be a shame to cut up to the edge of that lake and spoil the view looking at the mountain."

In 2006, after a spate of mergers and other transactions in the Maine forest products industry, the Gardner Land Company said that it was open to disposing of its 4,000-acre parcel.

Dunphy was enlisted to supply paintings to be given out as favors to major donors to a fund-raising campaign for the deal. She traveled to meetings with big supporters in and out of state. There was press. There were exhibits. "It was a fantastic experience," she recalled.

She donated some prints, and she also joined eighteen other painters in an auction of their painting services. The auction brought in $27,000— a droplet in the bucket for one of the biggest exercises of conservation philanthropy in New England history. In the space of a little more than a year, the state government and 1,000 individual donors came up with $14 million to buy 6,000 acres of forested lands and transfer their ownership to the Baxter State Park Authority.[67]

The painters brought more than money to the campaign. "It was the painters that brought attention to it," said Karin Tilberg, the state official who had enlisted Dunphy. As for Dunphy herself, she was given a chance to be part of something that personally meant a lot and from which she otherwise would have felt excluded. "Like a lot of people," said Dunphy, "I can't write a big check."

A CERAMIC BRICK MAKES A DIFFERENCE

In 1972, Huey D. Johnson founded the San Francisco-based Trust for Public Land, a nonprofit group that over the years has helped preserve millions of acres of land throughout the country, including the lands around Katahdin Lake in Maine. Johnson, a Californian, has also been president of The Nature Conservancy, the big environmental group. He's worked in conservation internationally, for which he's been saluted by the United Nations. Now in his eighties, he runs the Resource Renewal Institute, a nonprofit center in northern California that focuses on climate change, among other subjects.

Between 1978 and 1982, Johnson was secretary of resources in the first administration of California governor Jerry Brown during which his responsibilities included management of water policy, oversight of parks,

---

67 In 2012, the family behind the logging company donated 143 acres on the edge of the lake to the state; the gift represented the last privately-owned property on the lake's shores.

and the smooth functioning of a workforce of 14,000 employees. "I had a new problem on my desk every fifteen minutes," he recalled recently.

Early in his tenure a package arrived in the mail that contained a colorful porcelain brick. On one side were the handprinted words "Save Mono Lake." On another side were instructions about how to place the brick in the back of a toilet so as to reduce the amount of water that was needed for flushing, a do-it-yourself low-flow toilet. Another side carried a reflection that said in part: "One brick in every Los Angeles toilet tank could save Mono Lake."

Johnson knew about Mono Lake. At 45,000 acres it was the second-largest body of water in California and also, through diversions of water from streams leading into it, a major supplier of water to Los Angeles 350 miles away. The diversions had been going on since 1941, and the effects were beginning to worry people who lived in the area. The lake was shrinking, salinity and alkalinity levels were rising, and birds were dying. Further, brine shrimp, a unique species, were disappearing with the effect of disrupting the food chain and threatening the economics of a commercial fish food industry. In addition, freshwater creeks downstream of the diversions had gone dry.

In 1979, people living around the lake and the Audubon Society, along with other environment groups, sued to stop the water diversions. Johnson knew about all that. He had previously backed various environmentalists' projects in area but he recalls today that he hadn't considered actually doing anything regarding Mono Lake until the brick showed up. "This one intrigued me," he said. The brick sat on his desk day after day, and eventually he got together with his people and convened a task force to look into the situation. This led to a series of public meetings around the state, during which water officials from Los Angeles were summoned to explain their water diversion practices in front of an increasingly interested population of environmental activists.

The proceedings didn't go well for the Los Angeles people. Johnson vividly recalls the moment when a lawyer for the city approached him at the end of a long hearing on a sweltering day, perspiring heavily, and saying, "You lucky bastard. I wish I was on your side."

In 1982, while the lawsuit against Los Angeles' taking of water was still being heard, Johnson appeared before a congressional subcommittee

on parks and public lands where he argued that Los Angeles really didn't
need to suck up so much water. He testified that the rapidly growing city
could reduce its use of Mono Lake water through better conservation,
among other steps. "The Department of Water and Power," he testified,
"is a captive of a cornucopian philosophy which assumes that there will
always be more."

The following year the California State Supreme Court ruled that the
water requirements of the city of Los Angeles should be balanced against
the diversion's impacts on the environment and public recreation.[68]

Antonio Rossmann, the lead lawyer for the Mono Lake interests,
credits the court ruling partly to the task force hearings that Huey
Johnson had held around the state. "The report [from the hearings] was
instrumental in providing the only factual account on which the California
Supreme Court relied to set the context for declaring a public trust in the
stream waters feeding Mono Lake," he recalled in 2014.

For his part, Johnson credits the ceramic brick that arrived in the mail.
In an account of the experience, he wrote, "I doubt the outcome would
have gone our way had the brick not been put on our desks."

Nor would Los Angeles have likely ever cut back on its diversions of
water from the Mono Lake streams and launched strict water conservation
measures, including giving away free low-flow toilets to city residents. As
a result of those moves, water levels in Mono Lake began rising.

The ceramic bricks—about twenty in all—had been made by Deborah
Small, then a ceramics student in her 20s at the University of California
Irvine. A native of Ohio, she had left a nascent career in occupational
therapy to go to California to study pottery, and it was there that she met
people who introduced her to the Sierra Nevada where she went hiking
and, in the process, saw Mono Lake—a place of remarkable beauty, with
otherworldly limestone formations and deep colors of blue, whose name
comes from the Native American Yokuts language—and she heard that it
was disappearing. "There was a committee that was already formed and
fighting," she recalls. "I remember hearing about the lake and what was
happening to it. I thought this is incredible what's happening!"

She heard about Los Angeles people putting bricks in the backs of

---

68 The landmark Mono Lake ruling extended to small streams a principle that dates back to
Roman times: that the government holds lands and waters in trust for the public and that it must
take into account competing claims about how those lands and waters are used.

toilets in the cause of saving Mono Lake. But conventional clay bricks are prone to disintegration, and so Small designed a ceramic substitute that wouldn't fall apart—not to be put in the backs of toilets, actually, but to be symbolic—and she picked out the names of twenty public officials. She sent each of them a brick, paying for the postage from a part-time job. She'd asked the college to help with the postage, but the college told her that her project was too political to qualify for funding. Instead, as she recalls it, "the college people called in the media. I was in the papers. I was on TV. It was a little crazy."

In time Small went on to other things. She's since written about sexual violence. She's written about the cultural traditions of a dozen native plants. She published a book about the colonization of North America titled *1492: What Is It Like to Be Discovered?* She teaches art at the college level, and she says that one of her messages for her students is that even young people can make change happen.

She and Huey Johnson have never met. But the relationship continues in a fashion. Thirty-five years after she mailed him the brick, he says he's still got it in his office.

Chapter 10

Fish Stories

The invasives and the migrators

≋ ≋ ≋ ≋

WHEN NEW SPECIES SHOW UP

Ice fishing is a big deal in Maine. Every winter 68,000 people spend close to $50 million on food, fuel, lodging, equipment, and bait for an experience that most Americans can't even imagine. In a northern state that's dotted with literally thousands of lakes and ponds, fishing through a hole in frozen water is an indelible part of the identity.

For quite some time, Robert J. Taylor supplied some of those cold-weather anglers with live bait from a business that he ran in Orono, a college town thirty miles up the Penobscot River from the Atlantic coast. Taylor annually raised up to two million baitfish called golden shiners on his seventy-acre farm, but on a December day in the early 1980s, apparently sensing that he was going to run short, he contracted with a company in Connecticut to supply him with 158,000 of the three- to four-inch-long baitfish. He never took delivery; authorities confiscated the shipment of minnows at the state line.

A little more than twenty years earlier, in what's believed to have been a first in the nation, the Maine legislature passed a bill that prohibited imports of live bait. Lawmakers at the time were worried that a parasite that had infected baitfish in neighboring New Hampshire might somehow wind up in Maine's inland waters and ultimately disturb the health of the state's iconic wild fisheries.

Taylor, who died in 2009, put the confiscation and the associated $6,000 fine and the prospect of jailtime in personal terms. He complained to an Associated Press reporter that he'd been a victim of character assassination whom authorities were trying to bully into prison. But this case was larger than a single man and a shipment of bait across state lines; the case, which remains a subject of study at law schools for the US Supreme Court ruling that it led to, was about the defense of a state's native and natural resources.

This book so far has been about the impact that humans have on and around fresh water, whether that involves using it, abusing it, diverting it, protecting it, or cleaning it up. This chapter is about something else. It's about the influence of human hands, accidental and otherwise, in determining what lives in rivers, lakes and ponds.

That's no small thing. Consider, for example, what one aquatic weed has done to fresh waters in North America after it was unwittingly introduced by humans. The weed is called Eurasian watermilfoil. It's believed to have crossed the Atlantic Ocean sometime between the nineteenth century and the 1940s, either in the ballast of ships or as decorative foliage in aquariums. The feathery plant forms mats of vegetation and tangled growths in lakes and ponds that can crowd out native plants, inconvenience swimmers, clog the propellers of motorboats, provide habitat for mosquitoes, reduce the value of lakeside properties, and turn off tourists. Milfoil, which is now in the waters of most states and Canadian provinces, is an unwelcome visitor that's tough to evict. It can cost up to $2,000 per acre to poison the weed and nearly as much to remove it by hand. Government agencies have tried using weevils, moths, caterpillars, and carp to eat the stuff with varied results. The default strategy is to keep milfoil from getting into the water in the first place, for example, by getting volunteers to stand sentry at boat ramps on countless lakes to watch out for fragments of the weed on boat trailers. There's also public education, which in Maine includes sticking reminders on motorboat registrations that read "Stop Aquatic Hitchhikers—Preserve Maine Waters."

As for invasive fish, that's a bit more complicated because at one time or another government officials consciously deposited nonnative fish into local waters. The idea was primarily to improve the fishing experience with variety, only then to learn that nonnative fish can wind up infecting natives with disease, or competing with them for food and habitat or, rudest of all, eating them. The Maine law that blocked imports of baitfish was aimed at avoiding such outcomes, and rightly so according to the Supreme Court's decision in the baitfish case in 1986. Writing for the majority, Justice Henry Blackmun agreed that, ordinarily, interstate commerce was protected by the Constitution, but he added that some things were more important than trade, in this case the protection of a state's environment from possibly irreversible harm.[69]

69 Maine v. Taylor, 477 U.S. 131 (1986).

The Maine law that was at the heart of the baitfish case reflected an early awakening about invasives. The credit for that awakening goes to Charles S. Elton, a British zoologist. In the 1950s he wrote "The Ecology of Invasions by Animals and Plants," a landmark study that for the first time catalogued the many ways that humans had shifted nature around for their own purposes, and not only to enrich the fishing experience. An unusually ingenious example was the shipment of an American minnow named *Gambusia affinis* to parts of the world where malaria's a problem. The tiny fish dines on mosquito larvae, hence its nickname mosquitofish. The minnow was native to central and southern parts of the United States where its appetite for mosquitoes was discovered, and by the time that Elton did his investigations it was the most widely distributed freshwater fish in the world. It's credited with having helped eradicate malaria in South America, and today it's being enlisted to go after mosquitos that carry the Zika virus.

Not everybody has good feelings about the mosquitofish, however. In Australia where the minnows were imported in 1925 to battle malaria, they're now considered a nuisance for their tendencies to attack other fish, plus eat the tadpoles of various frogs, plus consume plankton that otherwise can help keep algae blooms in check. Rather coldly, Australia's Biosecurity Act of 2014 lists *Gambusia affinis* as "a noxious fish."

The story of the mosquito-eating fish, valued by some and abhorred by others, is complex and conflicted, but it's hardly the only fish story that has two sides. You don't have to look hard to find other examples, even to one of the most celebrated and romanticized fish in the American consciousness: the eastern brook trout.

Perhaps more than any other fish, brook trout stir a sense of connection to a paradise lost where an ordinary person, no matter his or her calling or background or economic well-being, can get in touch with peace, harmony, humility, even divinity.

Gale Russell, an older man down the road from me, lives near a small granite dam on Roaring Brook. The dam, which was built to supply drinking water to neighborhoods several miles away, went out of service decades ago, and its impoundment area is now filled with silt. The water in the small pond is no more than a foot or so deep, shallow enough to be warmed by the sun and unlikely to appeal to fish species that prefer cold conditions. In Russell's long experience the brook that flows up to the dam has never had trout in it. Perch, yes, sunfish, yes, catfish, yes. Fish & Game has never stocked the stream, but the brook is so bucolic in its passage through the woods that it's hard to imagine trout not swimming there. Russell says that he's seen people drive up to the gate that blocks the forested road to the dam and then get out with their fishing gear and exclaim, "Oh, I'm going to catch a big trout!" He has a good laugh when he tells the story and then says with mirthful conviction, "It's not going to happen."

But in fact there are places where brook trout do swim, and remarkably that includes waters that are thousands of miles away from the species' native environment in the East.

The setting is Colorado, rocky and wild. In the early nineteenth century, streams and rivers there supported rich supplies of native fish, memorably cutthroat trout. But settlers did a number on the environment in an anything-goes economic expansion. They filled streams with residues from mining, sawdust from wood mills, and waste from cattle ranchers. Clear-cutting of forests left streambanks eroded and streambeds filled with sediment. Populations of cutthroat trout, over-fished in some places, shrank perilously. In the 1870s, after the science of fish culturing had made gains, Coloradans started importing nonnative fish to put in local waters. They brought in rainbow trout from California and brown trout from Europe and eastern brook trout from New York.

There were consequences. Not all trout are alike or even compatible. Stocked rainbow trout, for example, bred with cutthroats to produce a genetic mongrel that didn't adapt well to local conditions. Brown trout attacked the native cutthroats. And brook trout, with their early spawning patterns and particular eating habits, left little food for native fish to eat.

By the late 1930s, Colorado's greenback cutthroat trout were said to be near extinction. There were restoration efforts, but mistakes were made— for years fisheries people hatched and stocked the wrong subspecies of cutthroat, earning them headlines that included the word "Whoops!" In a hopeful move in 1994, Colorado adopted the greenback cutthroat trout as its state fish, but today that fish in its genetically pure form occupies less than one percent of its native range, due in part to invasives that were brought in from afar.

Meanwhile, in a cruel comeuppance, brook trout in their own native waters have been facing hard times themselves. Long ago brookies filled rivers and streams in much of the Northeast, but naturally reproducing populations of the wild fish are now pretty much confined to only a few hundred lakes and streams, most of them in Maine. Humans had a hand in the wild species' decline, first through overfishing and then logging, dam-building, farming and other activities that filled streams with silt and pollution and that also raised the temperature of waters beyond what trout could stand. Then, in the cause of better angling, humans introduced nonnative fish that either ate the natives or crowded them out. Bass, which were introduced in Maine in the 1860s, prey on young trout, as do other nonnatives such as pickerel and northern pike and muskellunge that now swim in Maine waters.

People have known about the dangers of mixing fish for quite some time. The annual report of the Maine Fisheries Commissioner in 1867 included this caution: "[T]he legislature should forbid the introduction of pickerel into any waters where they do not now exist."[70]

Still, introductions of nonnatives kept on, as did worries about the consequences. In 2005, the Maine state legislature put limits on stocking any kind of fish, including even hatchery-raised fish, in certain local waters. The goal was to protect wild fish populations from disease and parasites that nonnatives might be carrying, and also to keep the natives' gene pools pure—and not just in the waters where nonnatives are deposited. Introduced fish can eventually escape the waters where they've been stocked and find their way to other waters through connected streams and rivers, effectively altering Eden one pond at a time. Not everyone worries about such things, but others do, as the following experience will show.

In August 2015, a team of Maine state fisheries biologists on a routine sampling job examined trout in Mitchell Pond in the small community of Dedham. The fish struck them as having the look of hatchery-raised brook trout, which was a surprise because the thirteen-acre pond was off-limits to stocking.[71]

---

70 The quote appears in a report titled "Chain Pickerel Assessment" by Ronald K. Brokaw for the Maine Department of Inland Fisheries and Wildlife Divisions of Fisheries and Planning, 2001; updated by Jim Lucas, 2008.

71 By being more than ten acres in size, Mitchell Pond was subject to the "law of great ponds," a legal concept from early English common law that signifies that the pond was held in trust by the state for public use; the state of Maine did not permit the stocking of fish in the pond.

The biologists reported their finding to the state warden service, which after a bit of research theorized that the hatchery fish had been put in the water by the owner of the only house on the pond.

Nine months later, after monitoring sales of permits for hatchery-raised trout, a team of wardens tracked the homeowner as he drove a dozen miles to the city of Bangor where he picked up six boxes containing a total of 300 brook trout at a government office. According to the permit that he had applied for, the man was then to drive to the town of Orrington not far away where he would dump the hatchery fish into a private pond. But he didn't drive to Orrington; instead, he returned to his home where he backed his pickup to the water's edge where a couple of workers began dumping his $600 worth of the hatchery-raised brook trout into Mitchell Pond. At that point, the wardens presented themselves. Seated in the cab of his pickup, the man blurted, "You got me."

He had by his own admission previously stocked the pond with hatchery-raised fish without getting caught. In fact, he bragged that he was the reason there were trout in Mitchell Pond in the first place. Later in Hancock County Court in Ellsworth, Maine, the seventy-two-year-old man was convicted of stocking inland waters without a permit and was fined $1,000.

The full file for the case makes for some dramatic reading. The record includes multiple wardens' observations from different angles during the stages of the investigation, the sleuthing, the tailing of the pickup, and finally the catching of the guy in the act. The report reads like the script from a detective show, and it includes a telling statement by the man at moment he was accosted by the wardens—a statement that confirmed that not everyone's on the same page when it comes to native species. "Aside from breaking the law," the man asked the warden, "what am I really hurting?"

MIGRATING FISH AND US

In August 2017, a fisherman on the Connecticut River in southern Vermont reeled in a living relic from the prehistoric past. It was a shortnose sturgeon, a fish whose looks and potential size (some oceangoing sturgeon can run twenty feet long) have fueled sightings of sea monsters over the centuries.

Sturgeon have only one natural enemy. That would be us. We've eaten the fish and harvested it eggs for caviar despite Biblical orders not to ("They are an abomination for you" Leviticus 11:9–12). But pollution and blockages by dams eventually earned the fish a protected status, which explains why the angler released his catch back into the river and then notified government officials.

In a region that once teemed with sturgeon, the landing was big news. The National Oceanic and Atmospheric Administration issued a press release that was widely republished: "Surprise Catch: First Shortnose Sturgeon Documented Above Dam in Connecticut River."

There are several theories how that particular fish got to be where it was, upstream of power dams. Maybe somebody deposited the fish or an ancestor from someplace else; maybe some sturgeon got trapped there when the first power dams went up long ago; maybe the addition of passageways at downstream power dams was finally paying off. Whatever the cause, the spotting of the sturgeon was exciting, affirming, and good. It evoked early times when sturgeon were abundant and the river's waters were pure; the catch intimated a *return* to those times; it suggested the idea of recovery.

There've been other reports of recovery lately. The removal of dams on the Penobscot and Kennebec Rivers in Maine, for example, has led to the return of shad, herring, and other fish that migrate between salt and fresh water.

And in November 2015, a team of biologists in Connecticut came upon three nests of salmon eggs on the Farmington River, a tributary of the Connecticut River. The discovery presaged the first hatch of wild salmon in those waters since the Revolutionary War. The discovery was posted on FaceBook, and a photo of the undisclosed location went viral.

The report of the salmon nests was all the more exciting because, three years earlier, the federal government and states along the Connecticut River had pulled the plug on a forty-year multimillion-dollar effort to restore Atlantic salmon to the river's watershed through the use of hatcheries, the removal of dams, and the installation of fish ladders and elevators.

So, here, salmon were returning to spawn on their own! They had made their way up from the sea, past where a dam once blocked them, to lay their eggs naturally in clean water. "We were pretty excited," said Steve

Gephard, a fisheries biologist with the Connecticut state government who spotted one of the nests.

The stories of the sturgeon in Vermont, the salmon in Connecticut, and the migrators in Maine are uplifting and warming. They recall for us the plenty that awaited Europeans before they altered rivers in the name of progress. These stories, therefore, aren't only about fish. Each in its own way is also about humans and what they've done and sometimes tried to undo in and around rivers where migrating fish have come and gone and now, well. . . .

Human impact came early, even before Europeans showed up. Some years ago, archeologists came upon a V-shaped structure of stones in the Ashuelot River not far from where I live. The structure, one of the first such finds in the nation, was taken to be an aboriginal channeling device for harvesting fish.

In time, European settlers moved in, and in the course of time they built their own structures in the same river—not to harvest fish but rather to generate power for industry. The structures were called dams, and one of their effects was to block the passage of migrating fish, a disruption that led to strife as this history from 1892 recalls:

> "Salmon and shad ascended the Ashuelot River before dams were built across it. When the people found that their yearly supply of these fish was cut off by these dams, there was much complaint, and doubtless there were those who were willing unlawfully to engage in making free passage-ways for the fish through the dams. The General Assembly was petitioned during several years for redress in this matter, and January 15, 1789, an act was passed requiring a sluice to be kept open in every dam on said river in the towns of Hinsdale, Winchester, Swanzey and Keene, between the 10th day of May and the twentieth day of July in any year."[72]

That crisis over fish passage appears to have had a happy ending. Good for everyone. Here was the frontier, here was struggle followed by accommodation and resolution. Here were pioneers with conflicting priorities working things out.

---

72 Benjamin Read, *History of Swanzey, New Hampshire, from 1734 to 1890* (Salem, MA: Salem Press Publishing and Printing Company, 1892), 73–74.

Not all such conflicts over diadromous fish—fish that migrate between salt and fresh water—concluded that well, however. There was, for a particularly tragic example, the case of Chief Polin of the Wabanaki people in Maine in the first documented protest of a dam in colonial America. The conflict is worth a look because it wasn't between competing sets of people as much as it was between clashing concepts of nature. It was about whether the flows and cycles of nature should be left to run their courses or be interrupted by human design.

The story begins near a village of twenty-five families by the side of a river in southern Maine. The Presumpscot River ("Many rough places," meaning water falls) was integral to the life of the village. The river's flood plains provided fields for planting, the watershed sustained meadows and forests where game could be had, and the seasons supplied runs of migrating salmon, shad, and alewife.

In 1733, Thomas Westbrook, a British Army colonel fresh from the Indian Wars, turned his attention to logging. He picked a spot on the Presumpscot River for a lumber mill and set about planning a power dam. The dam would be huge, dwarfing the dams that beavers had previously built in the river, and so large and efficient that, unlike the beaver dams, it would block the passage of migrating fish. Local Wabanaki people complained about that. Their way of life depended on fishing, and their culture was guided by myths and stories about the troubles that can come from damming up rivers—the death of all fish and the end of civilization as they knew it, for example. Colonel Westbrook promised that he would install a passageway for migrating fish, but he never delivered.

In 1739, the local headman, Chief Polin, took his complaint to Boston where he told British authorities about how his people's lives had been upset. The official account of the meeting quotes him: "I have something to say concerning the river which I belong to. It is barred over in sundry places." He added, "It is [the] Presumpscot, which is barred up, and the fish is thereby barred, which is our food."[73]

The governor in Boston gave a listening ear. He was apparently

---

73 Excellent background on the struggle can be found in "The Reciprocity Principle and Traditional Ecological Knowledge: Understanding the Significance of Indigenous Protest on the Presumpscot River," by Lisa T. Brooks and Cassandra M. Brooks, in the *International Journal of Critical Indigenous Studies*, 3, no. 2, 2010, and also in a paper prepared by the Friends of Sebago Lake, the Friends of the Presumpscot River and American Rivers, September 2002.

worried that if tensions over the dam got out of hand there'd be more war with Indians. So he issued an order that the colonel allow fish passage during migration season, but nothing came of that.

At about this time settlers began moving further up the river to occupy lands that the Wabanaki people claimed were theirs. The pioneers set about building a meeting house and a power dam. The dam was destroyed by the native people, but other dams got built, and, in time, the Wabanakis left the area, returning only for intermittent attacks on dams, sawmills, and settlers.

In 1756, Chief Polin led a raiding party down the Presumpscot River to a spot near the new settlement of Windham. Hidden behind trees, he observed a farmer step out from his stockaded home. As the man entered a field accompanied by armed escorts, Polin took a shot but missed. One of the militiamen fired back, killing the chief. His clansmen carted his body away.

The incident is memorialized on the gravestone of William Manchester, the man who fired the fatal shot. The epitaph is there today in Smith Cemetery in Windham: "He killed in battle Chief Polin, May 14, 1756, ending the Indian War in this section."

The following years brought their own twists and turns. For one, white settlers began complaining about how dams were blocking migrations of fish. Still, more dams got built to power more mills, leading to economic expansion and its fruits: jobs, shops, wealth, pretty towns, and also fouled water, eroded stream banks, and fewer fish. After more than a century of this, new sensibilities and priorities brought new rules and laws that led to cleaner waters and the dismantling of dams. In 2016, nearly 300 years after the first protests about the blockage of salmon on the river, the owner of a power dam on the Presumpscot in the city of Westbrook, Maine, agreed to take apart its spillways and install fish ladders. The following year the advocacy group Friends of the Presumpscot River began raising money for a memorial to Chief Polin. Fittingly, the memorial's to be in Westbrook, the industrial city that owes its name to the dam-builder who ignited the fateful conflict with indigenous Americans so long ago.

Wildlife has been returning to the Presumpscot. Alewife and shad are swimming in its waters. The majestic salmon, the king of fish, can also be found in the twenty-five-mile-long river, although it's not the migrator that Chief Polin knew. The salmon in the river today are hatchery born. Since 1986 Maine's fisheries managers have been stocking adults near the uppermost reaches of the Presumpscot. John Waldman, a conservation biologist whose studies of migrating fish are among the best, has a sober take on that. Fish movements that result from hatchery stockings aren't the real thing, he writes. They're often "nothing more than sad relictual echoes of the natural abundances of the earlier pristine runs."[74]

No one today has any real hope that wild Atlantic salmon will once again swim up the Presumpscot, despite the removal of dams, the addition of fishways, and the improvement of water quality. For one, any imprint that would guide wild salmon to particular spots high on the river to spawn was lost long ago.

But wait. Several pages ago I wrote about the discovery of three salmon nests in Connecticut's Farmington River in 2015. Here was the natural laying of eggs on the gravelly bottom of the river—something that hadn't happened for centuries. Here was the first stage of a wondrous cycle that would next include the hatching of tiny salmon that would spend a year or two in those fresh waters, then migrate downstream to Long Island Sound, then journey up through 1,000 miles of salt waters to spend a couple of years off Greenland before magically returning to their natal place in the fresh waters of the Farmington River to begin a new generation of silver swimmers.

Who knows, that may well come of those three nests, but nobody I spoke with believes that anything approaching a real salmon recovery is in the cards in that river or most anyplace else in the Northeast. This, despite all that's been spent to end pollution, remove dams, add fish ladders, and design power-station turbines that don't cut migrating fish to shreds.

The fact is that the species' challenges today aren't in the rivers. They're mainly out at sea.

Rainfall in the North Atlantic is rising, and the melting of glaciers is putting more fresh water into the ocean. The result: a cascade of climate change consequences. Ocean currents are changing, and waters are warming. The warming waters have boosted populations of sea lice, a parasite that weakens salmon. The warmer waters have attracted predators

---

74 John Waldman, *Running Silver—Restoring Atlantic Rivers and Their Great Fish Migrations* (Guilford, CT: Lyons Press, 2013), 127.

that dine on salmon. Meanwhile, capelin, a fodder fish for salmon, have both declined in size and moved to different parts of the ocean. On top of all that, escapees from commercial salmon farms have spread disease to their wild cousins, weakening them for their long passages. Finally, factory ships—massive trawlers—have overfished the sea.

"It may not be just one thing," said Steve Gephard, the fisheries biologist who was part of the team that spotted salmon nests in the Farmington River in 2015. In a way the sighting was a reward for a man who since the 1970s has worked for cleaner waters and fewer dams in rivers. The new problems for salmon are beyond his reach out at sea. "There's not a whole lot that we can do," he said.

The numbers give no cause to think that things will get better.

There's a power dam on the Connecticut River in Holyoke, Massachusetts, seventy miles upstream of Long Island Sound. The dam's outfitted with a set of elevators that lift migrating fish up over the top during their spawning runs. The fish get counted, species by species. In the spring of 2016, more than 385,000 shad took the elevators, as did 35,249 sea lamprey, and 638 sea bass. As for the number of salmon that were spotted on the fish lift at Holyoke Gas & Electric's Robert E. Barrett Fishway that year? Three.

Incredibly, there's good news in these tallies, just not for salmon. In recent years other species of diadromous fish have been on the upswing: shad, alewife, sea lamprey, eels. They're the beneficiaries of spending and strategies over the years that focused largely on improving the conditions for salmon.

Take the American shad. Here's a fish with history. George Washington's encampment at Valley Forge was facing famine when an early spring run of shad supplied his troops with food. John McPhee, the prolific writer, wrote a book about shad, calling it "the founding fish." The official state fish of Connecticut is shad. There's an annual shad derby in Windsor, Connecticut. There's a shad museum in Haddam. There's an annual shad bake in Essex. As a dish, the fish is so flavorful that it doesn't need spices—a compensation for its vast number of bones. But for all these credentials, shad have never had the glow of salmon. There's never been a tradition of presenting the first shad catch of the year to the president of the United States as there was for much of the twentieth century for salmon.[75] There's never been a shad equivalent of the North Atlantic Salmon Conservation Organization or the Atlantic Salmon Federation or the Connecticut River Salmon Association. There's never been big money for shad.

"It's hard to get attention for shad," said Gephard. Still, that fish and the other migrators are recovering while, ironically and tragically, salmon are suffering; those migrators benefitted from the work done in salmon's name.

"[Salmon's] a romantic species," he said. "It's charismatic. It just captures our attention."

---

75 The history is the basis for *The President's Salmon: Restoring the King of Fish and Its Home Waters,* by Catherine Schmitt (Lanham, MD: Down East Books, 2015).

Chapter 11
The Citizens
How ordinary people have made a difference around water

$\approx\approx\approx\approx$

TESTING THE WATER

On a September day in 2016, Pat Young pulled up to the Blackledge River in rural Connecticut and got out with a bunch of nets. It was, as she remembers it, a gorgeous warm day, a perfect day for wading in and looking for insects.

Young isn't a scientist, but she knows that certain bugs can tell you something about a river, which is: if they're living in it, the water's clean; if they're not, it's not. Some bugs can't stand pollution. As it used to be with canaries in coal mines, aquatic insects can tell you that a river's clean just by surviving in it. Such creatures are called bioindicators.

Young works for the Salmon River Watershed Partnership, an alliance of towns and nature organizations that, since 2007, has been looking out for streams and rivers in southeastern Connecticut. The group's activities directly and indirectly include conserving lands, demolishing dams, inspecting culverts, and checking on the quality of water in local ponds, rivers, and streams.

She wasn't alone on that day in 2016. She was joined by about ten members of Boy Scout Troop 39 and their parents, on a mission to see whether this particular section of the sixteen-mile-long river, downstream of long-gone mills, could qualify as clean. The section was shallow and the bottom was gravelly, which assured a bit of turbulence—conditions that suit aquatic insects for the extra-oxygenated water and nutrients that get trapped amid stones.

The scouts jumped to work with their nets, and soon enough they pulled up four different kinds of benthic macroinvertebrates—that's bottom-dwelling bugs, to you and me. The findings landed this section of the Blackledge on a list of healthy rivers.

That's quite a story, Boy Scouts helping credential a river by the insects they find in it. The action helps illustrate where much of the work on behalf of rivers and streams gets its start. It isn't at the policy level where politicians and bureaucrats do their thing. It's at the grunt level where ordinary people haul out old tires on cleanup days; where they put together fund-raising campaigns to help buy watershed lands; where they argue for laws to keep pollution out; where they insist that old dams be taken down; where they go into schools to talk to kids about the health of fish.

This chapter is about people who care enough about the streams and rivers and lakes around them to make a difference:

- Every year upwards of 1,300 volunteers take part in cleanups, water sampling, and wetland restorations for the Rhode Island-based Woonasquatucket River Watershed Council, on and around a once-badly polluted waterway.
- In central Maine, members of the nonprofit Friends of the Cobbossee Watershed teach waterside property owners what they can do to prevent runoff into streams and ponds.
- Since 2003, volunteers from the Shadow Lake Association in northern Vermont have been washing down trailered boats with 140-degree water to keep invasive weeds out of the lake.
- In 2005, alarmed about polluting runoff, a group of residents in southern Connecticut formed a group they called Save the River Save the Hills to protect local waters from contamination. Among other things, the 400-member organization runs a boat pump-out station that annually keeps 6,000 gallons of sewage from getting into the water.
- In 2014, the Ashuelot River Local Advisory Committee in southwestern New Hampshire organized more than one hundred college students to pull 1,800 pounds of trash from local waters.[76]

---

76 The listed activities represent only part of what these groups do. See: Woonasquatucket River Watershed Council (http://www.wrwc.org/index.htm); Friends of the Cobbossee Watershed (https://www.watershedfriends.com/); Shadow Lake Association (http://shadowlakeassociation.org/); Save the River Save the Hills (http://www.savetheriversavethehills.org/); Ashuelot River Local Advisory Council (https://www.facebook.com/Ashuelot-River-Local-Advisory-Committee-260939780761660/).

No one knows precisely how many citizen organizations like these exist in the United States. Nicole Silk, head of the River Network, a national nonprofit based in Colorado, says there could be as many as 6,000. That's pretty impressive at a time when Americans are said to be withdrawing from civic life, not running for local office, not serving on the PTA, not joining up. But here are regular people—volunteers, not paid government workers—getting into the water one way or the other. It's work, but it comes with satisfaction, and it can come with a thrill.

"There's this whole fascination with bugs in the water," Pat Young told me, describing her excited Boy Scout water testers that day in the Blackledge River. "They never suspected that there's all that stuff in it!"

Testing water via insects in Connecticut began in 1999. The numbers of volunteers each year have run as high as 500. That's in addition to other volunteers who measure the temperature and salinity and oxygen in rivers and streams.

Water monitoring by citizens goes back to the 1920s, when the fifty-four founding members of the Isaak Walton League of America, a sportsmen and conservation group in Chicago, began complaining about sewage pollution of the Illinois River, a tributary of the Upper Mississippi. Within three years, the League had 100,000 members in chapters all over the place reporting back on waters that had been turned putrid by untreated industrial and human waste.

After testing standards and instruments reached certain levels of refinement, water quality data collected by volunteers gained some acceptance among experts. In the 1960s, the Isaak Walton League launched Save Our Streams, a citizen science initiative that enlists thousands of ordinary people around the country for water quality sampling.

Volunteer monitoring got another boost in the 1980s when the Environmental Protection Agency, reeling from budget cuts, began encouraging states to recruit members of the public to check on the water. In every state today, you can find ordinary citizens doing government-approved water testing. The EPA says that about 30 percent of rivers and streams in the nation are being monitored that way, which by deduction means that 70 percent aren't. Still, progress.

Over the years the character of water testing has evolved. What began as a general heath checkup expanded into more pointed exercises, for example, the deployment of volunteers by advocacy groups to spot the polluting effects of hydraulic fracking in a form of environmental policing.[77]

Well and good, but what I found to be the most compelling thing about water testing is that the main thing isn't necessarily what comes of the data that gets collected. The main thing is the consciousness-raising and environmental education that comes with it. Here, for example, is how the New Hampshire Department of Environmental Services introduces its volunteer water testing program: the purpose is to "promote awareness and education of the importance of maintaining water quality in New Hampshire's rivers and streams."

I got my first glimpse of just what that means not long ago. In the early summer of 2015, I accompanied a group of three volunteer water monitors on the lower reaches of the Ashuelot River, a sixty-four-mile-long tributary of the Connecticut River in southwestern New Hampshire. I connected with them following a training session at a local college where the volunteers got a short course in how to test water and also about how to dress out in the field to avoid ticks and poison ivy.

The team included a seventeen-year-old high school junior, her mother, and a college science teacher. The student, Madison Daniels, had chosen river monitoring as her senior project. She would spend the summer testing the river and then make a formal report at school shortly before graduating the following spring.

On a warm morning in June of that year we met in the parking lot of a drugstore at a rural intersection. The team's schedule that day included three monitoring spots, the second of which was on a state highway bridge over the river. We parked on the side of the bridge and, as we walked to the center of the span, Madison brought along a one-gallon plastic bucket that had a stone duct-taped to one side and a long rope tied to the handle.

She took her position at the bridge's midpoint, traffic whizzing behind her, and tossed the bucket into the river thirty feet below. I watched as the weight of the stone quickly caused the vessel to tip and fill up with water. She then hauled up the bucket and immediately spilled the contents out

77 See "What Is Volunteer Water Monitoring Good For? Fracking and the Plural Logistics of Participatory Science" by Abby Kinchy, Kirk Jalbert and Jessica Lyons (Bingley, UK: Emerald Group Publishing, 2014). http://kirkjalbert.com/wp-content/uploads/2014/07/Kinchy_etal_ PluralLogics_PPST_2014.pdf

onto the pavement. She repeated the process, hoisting another bucketful and spilling out the water again. Confident that the bucket was thoroughly washed out, she dropped it off the bridge again, this time to collect her usable sample. She hauled it up, and then she and her mother and the college science teacher and I walked the fifty yards back to our cars to get to the testing equipment.

Madison was new to water testing. She'd taken biology and chemistry at school, but she was no science geek. When selecting her senior project, which by design had to have some sort of community dimension, she'd considered running a sports clinic for kids. She was a three-season athlete (the day we met she was wearing her softball jacket). But she was also interested in the outdoors; she'd been on outings with the fish and game club, and a former teacher with whom she'd fished the Connecticut River suggested that she try water testing, and that seemed interesting.

The actual testing by the side of the bridge required a bit of concentration as there was a certain amount of instrument calibration to be done. There were some liquids to be added and a variety of observations about the color and smell of the water to be taken in addition to the actual measuring for algae, e-coli, temperature, dissolved oxygen, alkalinity and acidity, and so on. There was a lot of note-taking.

After the morning's sampling was finished, the team took the equipment and record books to the home of the local organizer of water testing, after which the data would be sent off to the state capital for analysis and storage. We parted there.

Eleven months later I met up with Madison again. She had invited me to serve on a panel for her senior presentation. The corridors of the high school that day were bustling with excitement and formality with teens in suits and dresses. In a classroom facing a panel of three men, Madison was poised, prepared, and well-spoken. She described what she'd learned about the composition of water and the importance of accuracy in recording what she'd seen. I asked her whether she thought that the experience might be of any use down the line after she graduated. It might, she said, and in a way it did. A year and a half after her senior presentation, I got back in touch with Madison again. She reported that she was now working as a dental assistant, and it turned out that one aspect of her work for which she said she felt prepared was that she had to test the water that's used in the practice.

My strongest memory of Madison goes back to something that she said at her senior presentation. It was about the awareness-raising aspect of her work. I asked whether she'd noticed any impact from the water testing beyond what she herself had experienced. She gave it a thought and replied, "Well, now my friends ask me a lot about water."

≈

But does any of this water testing have any practical impact? The answer is: It can, and here are two examples.

The Ashuelot River where Madison Daniels did her water monitoring is rated Class-B today, meaning swimmable and fishable. That's not always been so. Older locals can distinctly remember when the river stank of sewage and when the color of the water on a particular day depended on what the local mills upstream were doing. By the late twentieth century, the river was pretty much cleaned up, but looks aren't necessarily everything.

About a decade before Madison took her turn as a water sampler, earlier teams of volunteers on the same river began picking up high levels of phosphorous. Phosphorous, a chemical element, is essential for plant life, but too much of it can be a bad thing. For example, it can promote the growth of algae that in excessive amounts can suck so much oxygen out of the water that fish and other aquatic life can't survive.

The detection of high phosphorous levels in the Ashuelot coincided with two developments at the EPA, one being a general heightening of concerns about what's called nutrient pollution and the other being the renewal of the discharge permit for the Keene wastewater plant upstream of where the high phosphorous readings had been taken. In the order of things, the Keene City Council was asked to consider spending millions of local tax dollars to upgrade the city's wastewater treatment plant. The water looked clean enough. Why spend the money? Donna Hanscom, the assistant director of Public Works for the city, told me that the data that had been collected by volunteers answered the question. "They were a big piece of convincing the city council on why they had to do it," she recalled.

I came upon a much more consequential case in a city on the other side of the state. In Chapter 4, I described a stream named Berry Brook in eastern New Hampshire that, until a decade ago, was fouled by stormwater runoff carrying in dog doo and lawn fertilizer and road salt and other surface contaminants. Today, however, Berry Brook is a national showcase for how to control urban runoff.

Credit goes to a lot of people, starting with a small group of citizens who, in the late 1990s, got fed up with the stink and trash in local waters, including Berry Brook. The group's members got their hands on water testing equipment, and their findings showed alarmingly high levels of bacteria in the stream. The group took its samples to officials in the state capital who then alerted the EPA. In an alignment of the stars that included an interested city hall, a stormwater research center at a nearby university, a couple of nonprofits, a public works director who was open to change, responsive federal and state agencies, and an energetic watershed coalition, change happened. The brook, now on a path to recovery, is a stopping point for authorities in other parts of the country looking for what to do about urban runoff.

"It was an amazing project," said Sally Soule, a New Hampshire state government official who was closely involved with the recovery of the stream. "And it was so perfect how it happened." By that she meant how it was local citizens who began to turn things around.

Granted, Berry Brook isn't a big stream. It doesn't stand out for remarkable beauty. There's no eye-catching stretch of white water, nor a particularly prominent passage through an open field. It's just a tributary stream of no seemingly obvious importance beyond what its restoration says about where change of a meaningful sort can get its start.

LOVING A LAKE

In 2004, Kathleen Weathers, an ecologist at the Cary Institute of Ecosystems Studies, an environmental research organization in Millbrook, New York, began a sabbatical at Lake Sunapee in west central New Hampshire. The lake ("Wild Goose Water" in Algonquin) had long been a vacationer's paradise, and in fact, that's how Weathers first got to know it during childhood summers at a family place there, swimming and playing on its shores.

Weathers recalls that she didn't have any particular research project in mind when she landed at Sunapee, although it was understood that the local lake association where she'd be based was interested in beefing up the science side of its expanding array of nature-education programs.

But Weathers soon found a research focus, or rather it found her when a few lake residents for the first time noticed blue-green algae on the surface of the water, and they reported their findings to the lake association. The reports set in motion a series of serendipities that over the next dozen years upped the profile of the nonprofit Lake Sunapee Protective Association among researchers of fresh water lakes. Weathers eventually returned to the Cary Institute, but she maintained ties to Sunapee as volunteer director of research, and in 2017, she signed onto a new federally financed study of toxic algae in Sunapee and other northeastern lakes.

More about that research later. More here about why Sunapee prominently shows up in lake science literature today. The answer lies partly in the lake association, an organization whose life story is a lesson in history. What started more than a century ago as a small group of disgruntled shoreside property owners eventually became an internationally respected educational, research, and advocacy enterprise with a vision that extends well beyond the lake itself, to a watershed of forty-eight square miles containing thousands of homes and multiple sources of potential contamination.

I had heard about the lake association, and I was drawn to what the history of this one citizen-run organization could tell us about how our thinking and behaviors around water have changed over the years.

There's no question that they've changed. Here's a clipping from a weekly newspaper in the Sunapee area in 1899: "Those desiring to dispose of their cats, dead hens, etc., should notify the Lake Sunapee Water Supply Company to see that they are properly disposed of, rather than have them left on the ice of the lake or thrown into its waters."[78]

Sunapee's not the only place where dead animals are no longer tossed into the water or left out on the ice. But behaviors around Sunapee probably changed earlier than in most other places, and that's due largely to the nonprofit Lake Sunapee Protective Association, the first environmental organization in New Hampshire when it was founded in 1898 and since then a model for citizen action.

78 *The Newport Argus-Champion.* May 5, 1899. Cited by the Lake Sunapee Protective Association.

The origins can be traced back years before the idea of a lake association ever occurred to anyone. That would have been in 1847 when railroads opened the 4,000-acre lake to city folk from as far away as New York. Tourists began showing up, camping parties took to the shores, spiritualists arrived, and armies of anglers found trout and landlocked salmon rising to the fly. Resort hotels and casinos were built, steam boats that could carry hundreds of passengers plied the waters, and the summer calendar was filled with water festivals, regattas, and carnivals. Meanwhile, water-powered mills on the Sugar River at the outlet of the lake fueled the local economy.

In time, away from all this clamorous excitement the sound of grumbling could be heard, significantly in the shoreside cottage of William Swinton Bennett Hopkins. An accomplished lawyer in Worcester, Massachusetts, Col. Hopkins (31st Regiment, Massachusetts Infantry, Union Army), had taken to summering on the lake, and in the closing years of the nineteenth century he had become alarmed at what was happening to the waters and their surroundings thanks to the operations of mills. He helped organize the lake association and drafted a legal challenge to the mill owners' practices. In August of 1898, he held forth at a gathering at his cottage, and he later set down his thoughts, some of which I'm excerpting below for their sheer eloquence and intellectual rigor. I've read these lines many times, and more than once have I slipped into channeling the author. You might try it: It's 120 years ago, you're looking out on a lake that's given you many lovely summers, you're surrounded by some like-minded friends, and you've got something to say:

> "The objects of this Association are not confined to the advancement of any one interest but of the great and growing body of shore-owners. They include the preservation of the lake from all kinds of pollution, the protection of its fisheries from running sawdust into it, the encouragement of the preservation of the beauty of its shores, as well as the regulation of the drawing [down] of its waters . . .
>
> "An equity suit was instituted by the direction of this Association to ascertain and fix the rights of the shore-owners against the manufacturers, so far as they

were in conflict, and so far as they could be reconciled
with each other. When the hearing to establish the
facts, so that the Court may apply the law, convened
here a few weeks ago, it was found that there was a
story being industrially circulated about the shores of
the lake to the childish effect that this Association had
as its only object to *ruin the mill-owners*. The limits to
which human credulity can be played upon have never
been ascertained yet, and, wonderful as it may seem,
this fable has obtained believers, or at least to draw
the purse strings of those who pretend to fear that our
humble efforts, if successful, will financially injure this
community . . .

"Whenever men enjoy mutual and concomitant
rights in the same matter there is bound to be some
friction. There is only one rule known to the law, and
that is that such rights are relative to each other, and
must be enjoyed relatively with reasonable adjustment
and regard for the rights of all. This is all we ask of the
manufacturers. We object to the Pulp Company's saving
trouble and money by using the lake as a storage place
for logs—in other words, for its mill yard until clear into
the low-water season and then running through rafts
where they can do the most injury to shore-owners and
navigation. We say, 'Store your own logs in your own
yard and get them there in the high water of the Spring,
but stop putting them through with a great wash of
water in the dry season.'

"These mills nearly all have auxiliary power by steam
already installed; if not, they should have. We say, burn
the coal, which you must burn sometime, at the time
when it will do the most good to your neighbor, and
use your water when it will do the least harm. This Dam
Co. has no right to raise a reservoir by flowage. If it
does . . . attempt to hold more water because unusual
Spring rains have been vouchsafed, it will undermine

and cause the fall of trees and fill woods and low shores with mud . . .

"I have said that this regulation of the drawing of water is by no means the only interest that we should subserve. In point of time it seemed to be the first to challenge our attention. As the population of these shores, as it is bound to increase, probably exceeding much of the large growth of the past, the purity of these waters is of paramount importance. The lake is the one jewel that calls in all here. The man who builds his house on a hill and does not reach the shore at all, were it not for the lake would not have built it there. Carelessness, even the slightest toleration of the introduction of impurity, will destroy the healthfulness of the region, repel the newcomer who should be invited and destroy the value of what we have already established . . ."[79]

Two years later at age sixty-three Col. Hopkins was dead, but his ambitions carried on. In 1904, the lake group lobbied the New Hampshire Legislature for limits on dam operators' fluctuations of lake levels. In time, the group went after pollution from steamboats and the silting effects of logging on nearby hills, and it campaigned for sanitary standards for homes on the lake's thirty miles of shore.

The record of what came after is an instructive history of citizen action; it shows how beneficial change doesn't simply happen but, rather, is made to happen.

In the 1950s, the association, still very much a property-owners group, paid an expert to test the water to see if it was safe to drink, a rare step then for a private citizens group. In the 1960s, the association began asking local towns to hire health officers. In the 1970s, it hired its first employee and ordered up more water quality studies. The lake was generally healthy, but with more homes going up, more roads being salted in winter, and more motorboats leaking fuel, the risks of pollution were rising.

In the 1980s, the group pushed for land use controls near the water's edge. In the 1990s, it began testing streams that flowed into the lake, and it started taking its message into schools.

79 Circular by the Lake Sunapee Protective Association. September 4, 1898.

At a certain point, the association began asking swimmers to keep an eye out for invasive weeds that had been showing up in other lakes and, sure enough, in 2001 the aquatic weed milfoil was spotted in Sunapee. Working with the state the group installed fiberglass barriers to trap the weed, and it trained volunteers to snatch up any of the vegetation that got through. As a result, Sunapee today is one of the few lakes in New Hampshire where milfoil—an aggressive, resilient, and fouling vegetation in waters throughout the country—has been eradicated.

In 2005, Kathleen Weathers, the ecologist from New York then on sabbatical at Sunapee, heard about an intriguing plan to link up lake research from around the world. The idea: one massive network of remote sensing devices generating data about invasive species and algal blooms and so on. On a visit to a water research center in Wisconsin, she saw an early version of a wired-up buoy that could collect all sorts of information about what was in the water. Later, when she told her colleagues at Sunapee what she'd seen, they engaged engineering students at nearby Dartmouth College to design a sensing buoy that could gather and transmit data about the air and water. That was the first in what's now a network of 120 sensing buoys on six continents, all constantly sending information into a database that researchers all over the world can get into. It's a remarkable use of technology.[80]

This book so far has been about how our priorities and practices around water have changed over the years. By extension it's also about how what we know and don't know about water has changed; the more we learn, the more questions we have.

Several pages ago I mentioned the discovery of greenish scum on Lake Sunapee in 2004. Most people know the scum as algae, and in some varieties it can be toxic. Symptoms can include rashes and nausea, and in the case of pets that drink it, death, which makes it more than an inconvenience in an area that counts on tourism and vacation rentals for much of its income. Cyanobacteria, the formal name of the most worrisome variety, is ordinarily a farm-state thing that's linked in part to fertilizer runoff. But recently it's been spotted in northeastern lakes, including, oddly, Sunapee, a lake where the natural chemistry

---

80 The organizing body is the Global Lake Ecological Observatory Network (www. gleon.org).

contains few of the nutrients that are normally linked to the problem.

The lake association brought its scientific inclination to an examination of the situation. It ordered up a boring of lake sediment to see if anything could be learned there, and found to its surprise that the cyanobacteria wasn't a new thing—it had, in fact, been present in the lake in the nineteenth century. The condition apparently comes and goes, maybe associated with human activity, maybe not, perhaps something that the biology of the lake was doing on its own and not a phenomenon that had an easy explanation. "It's a conundrum," Weathers told me. "It's a little bit challenging—and depressing."

Among other things, the discovery challenged the notion that everything that happens in the water—and, by extension, in nature generally—results from human action. Who knows? Maybe there is a human cause that we just can't see right now. Or maybe not.

There's one other important point here, which has to do with how that particular quandary regarding toxic algae came to light. It resulted from a test boring of lake sediment that was carried out by a private nonprofit citizens group.

Yes, government has a role in this. In 2017, NASA awarded a $1.47 million grant to Dartmouth, the University of New Hampshire, and the Cary Institute to find out why the Northeast has lately been seeing increases in toxic algae. The research will draw on an array of sources including satellite images and volunteer water testing for information about blue-green algae in 2,000 lakes in the Northeast. Among all those lakes, Sunapee will get extra attention largely because researchers already know so much about its waters. I take that as a reward for the lake association's early interest in scientific discovery.

The lake group has one other distinction. Earlier than most other such organizations its members came to see themselves in the mirror. That is, they determined that it wasn't just other people who needed to correct their ways for the protection of the lake, mill owners for example; homeowners on the shore had a responsibility, too.

June Fichter, the executive director, offered an example. Not long ago the lake association, worried about the polluting effects of runoff at a time of increasingly hard storms, outfitted its headquarters with rain-collecting barrels and a garden that was designed to soak up stormwater. It then began offering workshops to show shore-side homeowners how they, too, could help keep stormwater out of the lake. Property owners showed up, and not always alone. In the confident tone of someone who knows what success looks like, Fichter said: "People come with their landscapers, and they say, 'I want one of those.'"

SAVING A RIVER

This next story begins and ends with jars of water.

It's early September 1966, a little after noon in Fitchburg, Massachusetts, a medium-sized industrial city forty-five miles west of Boston. Three helicopters have just delivered Governor John Volpe, Lieutenant Governor Elliott Richardson, Senator Edward Kennedy, Secretary of the Interior Stewart Udall, and assorted other big shots to a crowd of more than 500 locals assembled at the airport.

Secretary Udall gets up and declares that a "great crusade for cleanliness" is sweeping the country, and he explains that it'll cost a lot of money to make things right. At one point a woman gets up and hands him a jar of water. It's a Mason jar, the kind you use to put up beans and tomatoes for winter storage. A photographer for the local paper snaps a picture. The caption on the front page the next day says that the water was from the polluted Nashua River that flowed through town.

Off to the side Governor Volpe leans over to Senator Kennedy, who's also been given a jar of river water. The governor, who has a jar of his own back in his office, unscrews the top and gives it a sniff. The governor exclaims, "Oh, your sample is not as good as mine!"

Later in the day back in Boston, Volpe signs a pollution abatement law, the first of its kind for a state. Confirming Udall's comment about costs, the Massachusetts Clean Waters Act provides $150 million for water cleanup, a sum that today would amount to more than a billion dollars.

Much of what you just read had to do with the woman in the photographer's picture, the one handing a jar of filmy water to the nation's top environmental official. It was she who encouraged the delegation of government officials to stop in Fitchburg that day. It was she who enlisted hundreds of local government officials and business executives and ordinary citizens to be there. It was she who earlier in the summer had showed up in the governor's office with a jar of putrid Nashua River water and a petition with 6,287 signatures on it that called for passage of the Clean Waters Act.

Marion Stoddart had recently moved from the West to a Massachusetts town where, in her mid-thirties, she found herself cooped up in an unfamiliar place with children at home and not much to do. She got a taste for community action through a local League of Women Voters land conservation project, and at that point she began thinking about getting the government to buy land along rivers. She pictured greenway corridors made up of land that nobody at the time seemed to want and that could be had for not a lot of money. But everybody told her that there was no government money for buying up land, particularly on the sides of stinking rivers. It was at about this time that she joined the new conservation commission in the small town of Groton, Massachusetts, and that's when and where she began to focus not so much on the land that was on the sides of rivers but on the quality of the water that was in the rivers themselves.

It was a time of awakening about the environment. Rachel Carlson's "Silent Spring" about the harm from pesticides had just come out, and people were talking about how humans had mucked up Nature generally and, locally, the Nashua River in particular. In fact, people had been talking about the Nashua River for quite some time, for the raw sewage that went straight into it and the pollution from paper mills that had turned it so foul that, as one unhappy family put it, "You'll need a gas mask if you come to town."

- In 1936, a report by the Works Progress Administration, a Depression-era jobs program, declared, "There's no question but that the Nashua River is polluted."
- In 1954, a regional government agency said that the river was "outstanding for its worthlessness as a fish stream."
- In 1964, government biologists found that the only things living in the river were pollution-loving sludgeworms and midgeflies because the water was too wretched to support any other forms of life.
- In 1966, a local government official wrote the following to Senator Kennedy: "A wide selection of colors is available in this highly polluted stream as it meanders its way through Leominster and

the surrounding towns, and the coloring in this water will change almost as fast as the weather here in New England."

• Early in 1966, 600 residents in the town of Hollis, New Hampshire, petitioned their state's governor to stop the pollution of the river. They complained that the stink was so bad that they couldn't sleep at night. But most of the pollution was happening in Massachusetts before the river flowed north into New Hampshire, and so the head of the new conservation commission in Hollis sent letters to a handful of communities in Massachusetts and asked them to do something about the situation.[81]

The letter clicked with Stoddart. "When we heard what Hollis was doing, I decided I would switch my effort from protecting land to cleaning up the river," she told me.

She began going door-to-door talking to residents about the river. She approached people in shopping centers. She talked to local government officials and businessmen and newspaper reporters. She told them about a bill that had been filed in the state legislature by a local senator that would set up a division of pollution control that could require sewage treatment and give ordinary citizens a say in the health of rivers. She asked people to sign a petition that supported the bill, and she wangled a meeting with Governor Volpe to hand him the petition. She rustled up a delegation of local business and government leaders to accompany her to the governor's office, and she brought along a jar of stinking Nashua River water for him to keep. Here's what the petition said:

> "The message is exceedingly clear. Commonwealth officials and politicians should listen: The citizens in the towns along the Nashua River can no longer be pacified by descriptions of impending legislation, promises and generalities. They are quite tired of hearing politicians tell them about what is going to happen. Patience has been exhausted. The willingness to suffer industrial and municipal waste has run out. They will not be satisfied until pure water again flows in their river."

81 Much of the historical detail comes from *Report on Pollution of the Merrimack River and Certain Tributaries, Part V: Nashua River*, US Department of the Interior Federal Water Pollution Control Administration, Merrimack River Project-Northeast region, Lawrence, Massachusetts (August 1966).

Volpe was impressed. He promised that he'd keep the jar of water on his desk until the Nashua River was clean.

But not everybody was convinced that taxpayer-financed sewer plants or costly pollution controls at local factories made sense. In a documentary film about Stoddart's campaign for a cleaner river, a daughter recalls the anonymous phone calls at home that informed her, "Your mother's crazy, you know."[82]

There was also word that the manager of a paper mill along the river had told his employees that they had a choice: a clean river or their jobs.

She pressed on, both challenged by the job ahead and encouraged by the attention that her cause was getting. In countless meetings with local government officials and labor groups and business leaders and newspaper editors and ordinary citizens, she found herself speaking to an awareness that was already rising. William Flynn, the mayor of Fitchburg at the time, told a reporter for the *Christian Science Monitor*: "The thing that made me a real believer was when I got a letter from an industrialist which said, 'I came to your community with the idea of locating a facility. But after seeing your filthy river, I decided not to. Any community which allows an open sewer to run through the middle of town has so little regard for itself and its environment that I cannot in good conscience do business with anybody from Fitchburg.'"[83]

The Fitchburg mayor signed onto Stoddart's cause, as did a great many other locals to whom she'd pitched her vision that one day, if you could believe it, people might be able to swim in the river again.

And then Stoddart did a surprising thing. On the advice of her husband, she handed over control of her grassroots river-restoration effort to other people. In the place of the bootstrapping Nashua River Clean-up Committee, with a single energizing force, emerged the Nashua River Watershed Association, a nonprofit organization with a board of directors and members and money that shared her near messianic conviction that citizens could make a difference for the river and, ultimately, the land around it.

The part about the land was an important addition. In the early days,

82 *Marion Stoddart: The Work of 1,000* (documentary film). Written by Dorie Clark. Directed by Susan Edwards and Dorie Clark, 2009.

83 Catherine Foster, "One-woman crusade to rescue a forsaken river," *Christian Science Monitor* (July 21, 1987).

the group used a logo that affirmed that focus was on the river and its waters. The logo was in the shape of a "V" that represented the course of the Nashua River as it flowed southeast from its beginnings near Fitchburg to where it met its southern branch, at which point it turned sharply northeast toward New Hampshire.

The identifying illustration today isn't a "V." It's a horizontal wave of blue beneath a brushstroke of green. The defining focus today isn't a single course of water but an area of 538 square miles that, in addition to the river and several tributaries, also includes ponds, forests, roads, shopping centers and more than thirty cities and towns.

Much of the organization's work today is about the land in the watershed and what'll come of it. That means a lot of time with local governments and their zoning rules and land-use planners. "We're not against development," Elizabeth Ainsley Campbell, the executive director, told me. "It's a question of where to put it."

In a broad sense, then, the organization returned to where Stoddart had initially intended to go. Now in her nineties and still involved, she told me, "I knew in my gut, my heart, that to clean up the river meant we had to protect the land."

Along the way, the nonprofit association took up other subjects that were nowhere in sight in the early days—the arrival of invasive plants in local waters, for example, and the disruptive effects of some culverts on nature and wildlife. There was another important addition. The sole focus at the start was on the quality of water. Today, after intervening decades of suburban growth and changing rainfall patterns, it's also about the quantity. "Streams do dry up," said Campbell.

≈

I'm standing at the edge of the Nashua River as it flows south into Lancaster, Massachusetts, on a May morning in 2018. Looking downstream I see nature unfettered, unbuilt, and otherwise unbothered beneath a lightly clouded sky. It has the look of a nature calendar shot. The only incongruity is the faint sound of cars from the upstream side where Interstate-190 is carrying traffic to and from Fitchburg and Worcester over a bridge.

I'm with Bob Lidstone and Tim McGinn, volunteer water monitors for the Nashua River Watershed Association, whose findings on this day would be quite a surprise to anyone who knew the river back when Marion Stoddart started talking about it fifty years ago. Here's what Lidstone and McGinn wrote down on their reporting form:

> Water clarity: *clear.*
> Water color: *clear.*
> Odor: *none.*

Lidstone, a retired math teacher, recalls different conditions as recently as the 1990s that included flecks of toilet paper in local waters and the wafting stink of sewage.

But changes eventually came, most notably the disappearance of sewage and the opaqueness of the waters. The river's name derives from "Nashaway" that translates as "river with a pebbled bottom." When I was out with the water testers that day, I looked into the river and, yes, I saw rocks. Lidstone told me about other changes over the years, including the natural arrival of vegetation in the waters and then crawfish and mussels, and not long after that otters. Lidstone recalled, "Once the otters appeared, the crawfish and mussels disappeared."

The crawfish and mussels made a statement by their brief time in the river. They confirmed that change can be made to happen. The changes in the Nashua River came of citizen action, as did other changes in other waters described earlier in this chapter. In each case the recovery was moved along by government support, but in each case it began with ordinary people.

On and around the Nashua River, as in so many other places today, ordinary people are still at it. They pull invasive weeds out of local waters, and look out for runoff that carries pollution, and write checks to conserve watershed lands, and risk poison ivy to test the quality of river waters.

They do these things in the belief that otherwise little if anything would get done. And they believe that what they are doing can make a difference.

I can confirm that second point by looking at a Mason jar that sits on my desk—the same kind of jar that Marion Stoddart filled up with cloudy and fetid river water 50 years ago and then personally handed to political leaders. I filled up my jar when I was out with Lidstone and McGinn on that morning monitoring river quality. The water in my jar is clear. If I unscrew the top and give it a sniff, I smell no smell.

Chapter 12

Water Connections

≈ ≈ ≈ ≈

Forty years ago, some ponds in the East were as crystal clear as swimming pools. Not a weed in them. Not a fish, either. Clean? No. Those ponds were dead, poisoned by acid rain.

Many of those ponds have since recovered, thanks in part to emission controls at upwind power plants. The chemistry of the water has changed. The ponds, now supporting vegetation and fish life, are said approvingly to be "browning."

Until ten years ago it was common practice in some places to pull fallen trees out of streams. The idea was that a clean stream could speed stormwaters away. Then other experts said that downed trees should be left in streams because they can help check the damaging force of floodwaters, and the limbs and branches can also provide nutrients and homes for insects and other forms of life in the food chain. A healthy environment thing. So people stopped removing fallen trees from streams.

This book is about how humans have changed their ways around water, and the remarkable thing is how recent so many of those changes have been. Humans have been living around water for eons, yet most of this book has been about problems and practices and laws and technologies of only the recent past.

I know builders, for example, who not all that long ago filled in swamps and wetlands for their projects. That was before it was understood that swamps and wetlands, by soaking up rains and snowmelt, are good for flood control and water storage. There are laws against filling in wetlands today.

Forget new laws. There's also common sense. Between 1941 and 1951, to pick a particularly startling case, military trainees regularly dropped practice bombs on and near Quabbin Reservoir in central Massachusetts, the biggest drinking water reservoir in New England, as it was filling up. Sixty years later munitions inspectors came looking to see if there'd been any lasting harm. They found none. Still, nobody in government today would think of dropping bombs, even phony ones, around water that people are going to drink.

These experiences show that we're capable of changing our ways. That's good to know considering all the ways that need to be changed today.

Take intense rainstorms. Between 1958 and 2012, according to the government's 2014 National Climate Assessment, heavy downpours in the Northeast were up by more than 70 percent, the biggest increase in the nation. Meaning: more floods and more spending on flood repair and flood control. As I write these words, the two reservoir dams on the stream that's oft-mentioned in this book, Roaring Brook, are being reshaped at immense cost to keep from being swept away by a terrific storm. Improving dam safety to handle harder rains makes sense, and it makes even more sense to do something about the major underlying cause of those harder rains, climate change.

Then consider the impacts of modern science. Ever inventive, American businesses are constantly coming up with new chemicals that we either know little about or can't easily get out of waters that they leak into. I mean chemicals for industrial processes and wondrous consumer products such as nonstick cookware. Hundreds of those chemicals are unregulated, their effects on humans and nature unknown.

It was carelessness that got us to this point—doing things without much thought to the consequences. Carelessness is born partly of confidence that the world is in our hands.

Alexis de Tocqueville picked up on that confidence two centuries ago when he observed, "The American people see themselves marching through wildernesses, drying up marshes, peopling the wilds, and subduing nature."[84]

If de Tocqueville were to return today, he'd see better ways. He'd see laws that were written in the cause of environmental restoration and protection, and he'd see private citizens and organizations fighting to defend those laws when they come under attack. He'd see ordinary people putting time and money into thousands of lake associations and volunteer river councils for the purpose of cleaning up waters and keeping them

---

84 Alexis de Tocqueville, *Democracy in America* (1835), (New York: The Library of America, 2004).

clean. At universities across the land he'd find government-supported
research institutes that are looking into such things as water scarcity and
the role of clean water in public health.

He'd find, too, new sophistication about water and its problems. Not
all that long ago, water protection and water supply was mostly a public
works thing—better treatment, better distribution systems, and all. But
several years ago, after New Hampshire won $236 million from Exxon-
Mobil for polluting waters with the gasoline additive MTBE, the state
peeled off three percent of the court judgment not for clean-up and
new pipes—the expected thing—but to conserve land by the sides of
waterways. A pittance, three percent for watershed protection, but a start.

Returning to America today, de Tocqueville would find a rising
general awareness about our ways around fresh water. That, thanks to
organizations such as the Pacific Institute, a California-based research
center that puts out a Biennial Report on Freshwater Resources. Open
up its volume from 2014 and you'll find articles about people and
governments fighting over water access, the polluting effects of hydraulic
fracking, the expanding range of jobs in the water field, and the economics
of desalination. My favorite in that edition: a study of fantastical schemes
("zombie water projects" they're called) to shift water from one part of
the country to another, even one part of the world to another.

The rising awareness around water extends to the acknowledging the
cost of it. For decades, cities with public water systems kept their water
rates low either by turning a blind eye to leaks that needed repair or
by indirectly subsidizing water supply. That's no longer the case. Water
rates across the country are rising fast, so much that in 2017, Philadelphia
became the first city in the nation to base individual household water bills
on how much those households could afford.

Were de Toqueville to visit America today he'd find some important
lessons learned—if only learned by surprise. A decade ago, twenty years
after a serious local water shortage afflicted Brockton, a former industrial
city of 95,000 people in Massachusetts, a huge desalination plant opened.
Here was the future, never another shortage. But by the time the plant
opened it wasn't needed. The community and its people had since
replaced leaky pipes and installed new plumbing and put new water
meters at private homes to the effect of reducing the city's overall water

consumption, leaving the new plant a $100 million white elephant.

In a broad message, the outcome in Brockton showed that small individual actions such as reductions in household water use can be just as effective, perhaps even more effective, than a single big solution. That's an important lesson in a nation that's inclined toward big solutions: huge dams, giant earthworks, magnificent reshapings of rivers and zombie water projects.

In 2003, the New Hampshire Legislature raised the idea of taking all the treated sewage from forty communities on and near its Atlantic shore and piping the waste out into the ocean. The waste would have been cleansed to a certain level, yes, but the echo from the past was shocking. The echo was from the nineteenth century and much of the twentieth century when cities poured their sewage directly into public waters. In this case, the Big Pipe—that's how the plan was known—was rejected, a credit to common sense and environmental awareness.

The bottom line to the story of the Big Pipe, indeed the bottom line to this book, is that the story is as much about us as it is about water.

It's about our ability to change our ways and also to know to change those ways when we can and when we must.

A NOTE ON THE SOURCES

≈≈≈≈

During the course of researching *Water Connections*, I read a great many books, academic studies, and reports by industries, government agencies, and citizen groups. Only a small number of these materials are directly cited in the footnotes.

In some cases, the unreferenced source materials provided helpful context for my research, and in other cases they opened me to new areas of research that ultimately generated direct citations of other sources. One example is a paper titled "The New Deal versus Yankee Independence: The Failure of Comprehensive Development on the Connecticut River, and its Long-Term Consequences," by Eve Vogel, a researcher at the University of Massachusetts at Amherst, and Alexandra Lacey. The paper, published in 2012 in the *Northeastern Geographer*, the professional journal of the New England-St. Lawrence Valley Geographical Society, introduced me to the fascinating states' rights struggle over federal flood control ambitions in northern New England that's explored in Chapter 3.

Some other unquoted sources go unreferenced for being too obscure, one example being a seventeen-page typed report from 1940 titled "History of the Keene Water System 1868–1940." The report, which quite likely hadn't seen the light of day for more than half a century, was turned up in the municipal archives in the Keene city clerk's office by an industrious member of the city staff. The report was useful for describing the early back and forth over whether the taxpayers of Keene should spend money to develop a public water supply—a struggle that's relevant to a study about society and water.

As for books, I can't count the number I read in libraries, online, and at home. But I can point to some that were more influential than others in shaping my lines of inquiry and the structure of *Water Connections*, including those listed below. These and other readings helped prepare me for the principal source of research for this book, which was personal interviews with close to 200 people in and around water. I encountered them at water conferences, in fish and game offices, and public works departments; on the banks of rivers and lakes; in artists' studios; at colleges and at hydroelectric plants; at technology competitions and by the side of water supply dams.

≈ ≈ ≈ ≈

Conuel, Thomas. *Quabbin—The Accidental Wilderness*. Amherst, MA: University of Massachusetts Press, revised 1990.

A visually compelling report about the environmental consequences of a major water-supply project.

Cronin, William. *Changes in the Land—Indians, Colonists and the Ecology of New England*. New York: Hill & Wang, 1983.

A classic study of human impact on the American landscape.

Fagan, Brian. *Elixir—A History of Water and Humankind*. New York: Bloomsbury Press, 2011.

An extensive study of how water has shaped human society in different ways over thousands of years.

Fausch, Kurt D. *For the Love of Rivers—A Scientist's Journey*. Corvallis, OR: Oregon State University Press, 2015.

Insights into the connection of streams and what lives in them to surrounding lands.

Fishman, Charles. *The Big Thirst*. New York: Free Press, 2011.

An extensive commentary about the shortage, cost, and pricing of water around the world.

Fleck, John. *Water is for Fighting Over: and Other Myths about Water in the West*. Washington, DC: Island Press, 2016.

A confirmation that traditions, laws, and practices around water can differ sharply from one part of the country to another.

Gleick, Peter H., ed. *The World's Water—A Biennial Report on Freshwater Resources*. Oakland, CA: Pacific Institute for Studies in Development, Environment, and Security.

Every two years for the last two decades the Pacific Institute has published fascinating reports about the impact of human society on water.

Hunter, Louis C. *A History of Industrial Power in the United States, 1780–1930*. Vol. 1. Wilmington, DE: Eleutherian Mills-Hagley Foundation, 1979.
     Despite the imposing title, an easily accessible account of the evolution of waterpower.

Jackson, Daniel, ed. *Algae, Man and the Environment*. Syracuse, NY: Syracuse University Press, 1968.
     A wide-ranging study based on lectures presented at the NATO Advanced Study Institute in 1962 in Louisville, Kentucky.

Kempe, Marcis. New England Water Supplies—A Brief History. Boston: Massachusetts Water Resources Authority, 2006.
     A study of the evolution of water and sewer systems in one of the earliest settled parts of the United States.

Marsh, George Perkins. *Man and Nature: Or, Physical Geography as Modified by Human Action*. New York: Scribner, 1864.
     An early classic that expresses a timeless concern about human impact on the environment.

Muir, Dana. *Reflections in Bullough's Pond—Economy and Ecosystem in New England*. Hanover, NH: University Press of New England, 2000.
     A survey of the socioeconomic dimensions of water.

O'Neill, Karen M. *Rivers by Design—State Power and the Origins of U.S. Flood Control*. Durham, NC: Duke University Press, 2006.
     A deeply researched study of how humans have gone about engineering rivers.

Outwater, Alice B. *Water: A Natural History*. New York: Basic Books, 1996.
     A report about water ecology that has a national focus.

Pearce, Fred. When the Rivers Run Dry: Water—The Defining Crisis of the 21st Century. Boston: Beacon Press, 2006.
     An extensive study of water problems and opportunities around the world.

Postel, Sandra and Brian **Richter**. *Rivers for Life—Managing Water for People and Nature*. Washington, DC: Island Press, 2003.
     A challenge to the practice of trying to assure steady flows of water down a stream: "Floods are bountiful times in the lives of fish and other creatures living in large rivers and estuaries."

Waldman, John. *Running Silver—Restoring Atlantic Rivers and their Great Fish Migrations*. Guilford, CT: Globe Pequot, 2013.

An authoritative history of how humans have intruded on the movement of salmon, shad, and other migrating fish.

Zeedyk, Bill and Van **Clothier**. *Let the Water do the Work—Induced Meandering, An Evolving Method for Restoring Incised Channels*. White River Junction, VT: Chelsea Green Publishing, 2009.

An examination of new ideas about river restoration after floods have swept through.

ACKNOWLEDGMENTS

≈ ≈ ≈ ≈

This book was set in motion and guided to the end by scores of people, starting with my late parents Jessie and Jim Rousmaniere, who encouraged my curiosity, and also by my siblings John, Peter, David, Joe, Ned, Arthur, and Kate, who share with me the love of a good story.

I thank my former colleagues and copy desk editors at The Baltimore Sun for educating me in the importance of detail. I thank countless writers, certainly including George Perkins Marsh and other early environmental figures, for setting examples of clear expression.

Credit for my introduction to the ways of water goes first to the managers of the Peace Corps who assigned me to irrigation work in remote villages in southern India in the 1960s. For much of the current information about fresh water I thank a great many authorities, only some of whom are named in the text, who took my phone calls and knocks on the door, and gave me hours of their time.

I also thank the following individuals for helping shape the structure of the book: John Harris, Howard Mansfield, and Mary Ann Faughnan, my editor at Bauhan Publishing. For the design and promotion of this volume, I'm grateful to the rest of the team at Bauhan Publishing—Sarah Bauhan, publisher; Henry James, art director; and Jocelyn Lovering, publicity. And I thank my wife Sharon for enthusiastically supporting the entire project from beginning to end.

Finally, I thank the many citizens whose advocacy in the causes of stream recovery, watershed protection, and related activities gives this book a constructive forward tilt.